YOU ARE GOING TO PRISON

Jim Hogshire

Loompanics Unlimited
Port Townsend, Washington

You Are Going To Prison
© 1994 by Jim Hogshire

Cover by Nick Bougas

Published by:
Loompanics Unlimited
PO Box 1197
Port Townsend, WA 98368
Loompanics Unlimited is a division of Loompanics Enterprises, Inc.

ISBN 1-55950-119-7
Library of Congress Card Catalog 94-78105

Contents

The Criminal Justice Machine ◆ Pain ◆ The Loophole ◆ Flashing Red Lights ◆ The Brain of a Cop ◆ The Dilemma ◆ A Note on Sassing Cops ◆ The Smashed Door ◆ Calm Down ◆ Incriminating Evidence ◆ In the Squad Car ◆ The Three Rules of Criminal Law ◆ Ask Questions ◆ The Pee Wee Problem ◆ Be a Good Citizen ◆ Surrendering ◆ What to Wear ◆ Money ◆ Jail Life ◆ How to Behave ◆ No Exit ◆ Your Mouth ◆ Fellow Prisoners ◆ Bail ◆ Jumping Bail ◆ The Interrogation

Arraignment ◆ You Need a Lawyer ◆ How to Pick a Lawyer ◆ The Hearing ◆ The Prosecutor ◆ A Three-Pronged Fork ◆ The Mind of the Prosecutor ◆ Before the Trial ◆ The Plea ◆ Mitigating and Aggravating Circumstances ◆ "Rolling Over" ◆ On the Other Hand ◆ You Need Rehabilitating ◆ The

Introduction

Been breaking any laws lately? It's not too hard anymore. For years now, our society has been treating any social problem by making something illegal — or increasing government powers to control you.

Think your kid's not smart enough? Well, blame it on TV, then let the FCC have more control over the airwaves.

Scared of crime? Blame it on drugs. Blame it on guns. Blame it on foreigners, religious "freaks," communists, Arabs. Make 'em all illegal.

Of course, to enforce all this it's imperative to equip our police and militaries with the latest in lethal gizmos. To make sure they won't hesitate to use them, we've had to do away with constitutional protections (they're just loopholes for Arabs anyway) while broadening the scope of the government's "interest."

Still think you'll never be a "criminal"?

OK, how about "hate crimes," "conspiracy of one," mandatory sentences, pre-trial detention ... hell, write three bad checks, let the courts declare you a "habitual criminal" and put you away forever! In case you don't like someone and you see them once too often, don't forget your recourse to the crime of "stalking." Or maybe somebody's tired of your face.

But you're an innocent man .... OK, how about this law now in force in Wisconsin (and 19 other states) — mandatory arrest any time cops are called to a domestic dispute. If the cops get called to your place because an anonymous tip says you and your spouse are fighting, somebody's going to jail, or the cop loses his job. Once you're in jail, you're a criminal, pal, and you get no help.

Dig it, once this concept of mandatory arrest is fully accepted it'll be a cinch to expand it to everything else and then maybe we can get mandatory life for conspiracy to stalk with a mandatory death penalty if the plan was motivated by "hate" or occurred within 1,000 feet of a school! Imagine what they might do to someone who conspired such a thing three times ... while owning a firearm. Yikes!

The latest federal "anti-crime" bills being bandied around all contain upwards of fifty new capital offenses, including some that don't even involve killing anybody. Destroying government property by arson, for example, can get you the death sentence.

If breaking the law is easy, going to jail is even easier. The United States now holds more people in cages than any other country on earth. Both in terms of percentage of population and in terms of absolute numbers, nobody beats America. If your goal is to do time, you've come to the right country.

America now has more than one million, two hundred thousand people locked up in federal and state prisons. Another eight to ten million people each year pass through our jail systems. The magnitude of this is almost impossible to appreciate. The "War on Drugs" alone has earmarked $7.5 billion for new prisons and prison construction. Just for drugs. And just at the federal level.

A million people.

A half dozen people die each day in U.S. prisons. Another one hundred are seriously injured. Savagery and viciousness rule our prisons. Torture by prison guards is routine.

And if women feel the problems of rape and violent assault have reached intolerable proportions in the free world, consider the problems in U.S. prisons where sexual assault is a virtual certainty for anyone. For you.

You, the prisoner. One in a million.

Fucked up the ass, locked in a cell and eating fatback with hair growing out of it. Your friends will forget you, your wife will leave you, your mama can't help you and you will live by the law of the jungle whether you like it or not. That's prison. Hell on earth. And it is not a country club.

No prison is a country club. There are only two prisons in America that could be described as "not horrible." Both are federal prisons — one in Allenwood, PA, and another in Eglin, FL. There is no chance you'll be going there. And if you do, you will still get the shit kicked out of you if your sentence is any longer than 30 days — assuming you can keep on your toes for 30 days.

But mostly you'll be there for years. And prison will be in you for the rest of your life.

Let's party!

1
Custody

The Criminal Justice Machine

Perhaps the best way to view the criminal justice system is to imagine a huge machine with exposed rollers, cogs, and gears. Cross this mechanical image with something bestial and you see the machine also has clashing and gnashing jaws, and fly-paper tongues that snap out and act as conveyor belts. Maybe a big steel hole is the mouth of a strong vacuum. Inside you hear people screaming.

This monster/machine is so large you are forced to live near it. And you can do that. You can stand right up next to it and not get hurt — unless you become careless or unlucky. Then a ratchet arm may swing out and knock you against one of the rollers. Or you might curiously dart your finger between a couple of wheels just to see if you can get away with it. You may slip, grab the wrong thing, or get sleepy.

At that point the machine can hook you, begin dragging you in and nothing will be the same again — even though the machine may spit you out right away or you struggle free pretty quickly. Maybe you'll get out with a torn sleeve, maybe you'll never get out. One thing is for sure: It will be unpleasant.

Pain

This book is meant to be of some help to you in avoiding the pain that will surely follow your entrance into the machine. This book takes you from the time you see the flashing lights all the way to the electric chair, examining and evaluating every step of the way, looking for methods to make it easier on yourself — even to escape it.

The main thing is not to underestimate the machine. Any way you enter the machine, you can end up anywhere along the trail inside.

And don't think for a minute you can't be executed for not paying a parking ticket. The force of the law resides in its ability to kill you. If you resist the justice machine it will increase its pressure on you in steady increments up to and including killing you.

Refuse to pay your parking ticket and you are challenging the government. It will respond a little more forcefully than when you first broke their parking rule. It will increase the fine, pursue collection, send you a summons. Continue to refuse and they will become more forceful still. Eventually, law enforcement agents will pick you up. They may not go hunting for you, but if you fall into their hands (the red lights) they will use force to get you to comply with their demands. Resisting will cause them to drag you (literally) further into the machine. If necessary they will club you over the head, incarcerate you or shoot you. There are also other methods they have of dealing with you that you can't find in any law book because they are patently illegal — yet they happen all the time.

This book deals with all potentialities, not just those that are legally possible, though those are gruesome enough.

Because we're talking about the reality of the machine, I'm sorry to say that many things in this book are not backed up with ordinary sources. But everything here is based on the collective experience of lawyers, cops, prosecutors and prisoners — many of whose names you would recognize. It's all valid information, but, in the interest of truth, we cannot divulge the pertinent information to "prove" it.

Perversely, it may even be construed as a crime to divulge certain information, as it would essentially accuse the government of something unprovable in court. That would be a challenge and we know where that could lead!

You may choose not to believe some of what's in here, but we guarantee you that all of it is first-hand. There are no friend-of-a-friend stories, no urban legends.

A lot of this information is widely known anyway. Part of what we're doing is verifying what you've heard, debunking some other stuff and generally presenting a truer picture of what's going on — including many basics — so you can improve your chances of a quicker, less painful exit from the machine.

This is also definitely not a book on how to "beat the system." You cannot beat the system. This is a survival book. If you want to play David and Goliath, go ahead. This book is about how to save yourself — not how to destroy the enemy. Once you're snapped up in the maw of the machine, you're not in any position to destroy or even harm it very much.

This is also not a legal textbook. Although we discuss certain laws, what a law says and how it is applied are not related. The old saying about "you pick the law and I'll pick the judge and I'll win every time" may not be too inspiring for a high school civics lesson — but it's the truth. Which brings us to our first lesson.

The Loophole

There is no such thing as a "loophole." You will not be one of the millions the nightly news says get away on a "technicality." While there are isolated cases of people benefiting from certain applications of a law or ruling, these are people who have lucked out — they did not, and could not, plan it that way. Neither did the thousands of people now behind bars (or dead) who were wrongly convicted.

If you luck out, well, lucky you. But get your mind set for the real world, where it's just as likely to have bad luck as good — and the last thing you need is bad luck. What you need is to constantly look for ways to put yourself in the best position so you can, hopefully, save your ass — or at least some of it. So dump any idea of a *deus ex machina* coming to save you. The ACLU — in all likelihood — will not even hear about your case and even if they did, they wouldn't care. The governor isn't going to pardon you, and your friend who "knows somebody" probably doesn't.

Whether you are guilty or innocent is immaterial for the purposes of this book. You've been caught in the machine and society is about to show you the same compassion it shows everybody else who gets hit by the law. People who might otherwise sympathize with you won't help you. They'll will just turn the page in the newspaper and cluck their tongues.

Same as you do now.

Flashing Red Lights

It may not be lights in the rearview mirror. It may be a simple "Sir? Would you step over here please?" Of course it might be the sound of your door splintering under the boots of a dozen charged-up men with machine guns, screaming and throwing "flash bangs." Whatever it is, this is your signal that your finger has been caught in the rollers.

Really, your finger was caught way before this point. Cops may have been watching you for quite some time, listening to your phone conversations, photographing you, even bugging your house. You could be the victim of an anonymous tip or a "friend" who's rolling over on you. Or maybe a cop just noticed you and for some inexplicable reason, decided to stop you. They're not supposed to do that, but they do. Hell, it could be mistaken identity. That happens frequently.

In any case, your first contact with the police is a critical time. What you do now will affect your future both short and long-term.

At the point when a cop stops you, you are not under arrest, and that's important because as long as you're not under arrest you still retain some "rights" and the cop hasn't started any paperwork on you. If the encounter is fairly casual, a cop's natural desire to avoid work or other trouble works in your favor. Usually it will be sufficient to obey the guy. If you're having a party and the cop says you're too loud and to turn it down, then turn it down. If he says get off the table, do so.

A cop who detains you is allowed to pat you down for weapons. This type of search is limited to a superficial feeling of the outsides of your clothing (also your crotch!) to see if you've got a weapon with you. They cannot use this search to discover anything else. But they do.

Don't complain or express any emotion, and certainly not humor. Let the cop know he's dealing with somebody who recognizes his authority in the situation. This advice to essentially "kiss ass" is only good advice, since it increases your chance of getting away without much more trouble. (But see? It's already unpleasant.)

The majority of times a cop speaks to you it will be an encounter like this. It's very possible to be caught breaking some law or other and have the situation not go any further than the cop telling you to stop it. If that's the case, just obey and then get away from the cop as quickly as you can without pissing him off.

Do not laugh at the cop. Don't act like you think any of this is funny. In no way should you display "an attitude." Your Daddy may be the richest man in the county but if the cop doesn't know that it won't do you a bit of good while he's cracking your skull with a billy club. And even if your Daddy succeeds in getting the cop kicked in the ass, what good will that be if you get your head caved in? Worse, the cop could easily be a psychopath who doesn't care about your Daddy and beats the shit out of you anyway. Cops are not ordinary people, to say the least.

This leads us to another rule: You cannot beat a cop at his own game and on his turf. A cop is the most powerful man in the world when it's just you and him and you're not willing (and able) to kill him. The only way you can retaliate against a cop (or any other manifestation of the "system") is when you get to make some of the rules. By the side of a deserted road at midnight, you don't get to make any of the rules.

Acting cocky or otherwise antagonizing a cop may even serve to nullify your ability to retaliate later. Let's suppose the cop does some serious damage. At that point, the police department will be less willing to sacrifice that cop and admit they hired and employed a psychopath, because the publicity would be so bad. If the cop was merely rude, they might kick his ass a little bit. But if he breaks your neck, they are more likely to rally around him — and so will the prosecutor. Normally, in cases of police brutality, prosecutors don't even bring charges and it is never reported in the papers. Sometimes a prosecutor will call up his grand jury and get them to refuse to press charges. The Rodney King beating proved that even cops who are videotaped committing a crime will be let off.

And this is the case in every town, not just big cities. Rural county cops have been known to routinely torture and kill people they arrest. They have been caught beating prisoners to death over traffic infractions, and sodomizing petty thieves with billy clubs. This last-mentioned torture was recently doled out by a small town prosecutor while the local constabulary held the man down.

So while the cop has stopped you, bide your time. Above all, don't say much.

If you've been stopped in a relatively calm environment, try to keep it that way. Tell him your name and address (even though you are not required to) and perhaps a general description of what you are doing but do your best to say nothing more. Same goes for the pat-down.

This is pretty difficult. After all, if the nice man in blue asks you what you do for a living, why not tell him? If you've said you're on your way to your friend's house, why not give the address?

The answer is that you will incriminate yourself. Whether it seems likely or not, this is the first phase of an investigation and the cop, by asking you questions, is interrogating you. He or she is listening carefully to everything you say and you aren't going to outwit them. Cops have been trained for this and have got lots of practice, so don't expose yourself.

Another good reason to avoid conversation with a cop is that, depending on the circumstances, one or both of you is likely to get mad. Start getting rowdy with a cop and you are making grounds for an arrest. So even if the cop starts getting insulting, stay polite, stay calm. There's nothing to be gained by arguing or raising your voice. Also, try to disassociate yourself from anyone who's acting up. It's pretty horrible to get sent to jail because your "friends" are calling the cops names, etc.

But what if the cop starts beating the shit out of you anyway? You've got a couple of choices. One of them is to run. If you run, there's some chance the cop will pull out his gun and shoot at you. There's also a chance you could get away and stay free, especially if you've given the cop a false name, etc. But even if the cop knows who you are, you can escape serious injury and perhaps in the meantime, notify the press, the authorities, your lawyer, and everybody else what happened before they come to take you into custody.

If running isn't practical, then you should drop to the ground into a fetal position covering your head with your hands and start shouting, "I'm not resisting arrest!" If there is anyone else nearby also scream for help and ask them to call 911. Calling 911 can help you out later, as the conversation will be recorded and kept on file for at least three months. You may be able to use this tape later to demonstrate that you were a victim of police brutality. It may also bring more witnesses and/or other help to the scene.

But don't count on it.

The Brain Of A Cop

Keep in mind, from the cop's point of view, there are only two kinds of people in the world — cops and scum. They know they are feared (and therefore hated) by a majority of people and everything they hear and see reinforces that. Cop shows on TV always stress the supposedly peculiar circumstances of a cop.

The establishment line on cops says they are a breed apart, constantly in danger and never being thanked for the courageous deeds they do. Even a cop's family is considered different. After all, the wife of a cop "lives with the nightmare of not knowing whether her husband is coming home or not" (as if the wife of a convenience store clerk has it any different). It is a fact that cops do not arrest each other, nor family members of cops when they are caught committing crimes, whether that's drunk driving or burglary. Cops, stopped by other cops, need only show their badge to be let off. Laws are rarely enforced against the police by other police.

Conservative estimates find ten percent of cops are "corrupt," which means they have done something so bad even the establishment cannot ignore it. In reality that figure is much higher when you stop to consider that cops' private crimes are widely known but never reported by their police "brothers." At a *minimum* these silent cops are aiding and abetting what they know to be plain wrong.

So to make it all seem right in their heads they stick to the line that cops are different. Cops are allowed these "mistakes." They are not criminals, they are frustrated with the inefficient justice system and therefore act "extralegally." Hell, in the cop mythos, this is even encouraged.

Cops believe this "hero" bit. They know all they really ever do is cite people for watering their lawns on the wrong day or hand out traffic tickets. They know their chances of being killed on the job are far lower than a taxi driver's, but they still see themselves as heroes — the "thin blue line" between us ungrateful citizens and total anarchy.

So if a cop begins to talk to you, there's a good chance they think you're a criminal and will look for anything to support that belief.

The Dilemma

So there you are, not under arrest but not quite free to go, and the cop has, say, pulled you over for whatever reason (he's supposed to have one, but often doesn't, although he can make one up very quickly) and now he's asking you questions you don't want to answer and don't have to answer. If you answer, he'll use it against you (that's the only reason he's asking). If you don't answer, he'll see that as suspicious behavior and use that against you, perhaps placing you under arrest.

In this situation it's best to simply tell the cop outright that you don't want to answer any more questions and ask if you are free to go. If he says you are, then bid him good day and quickly leave the scene. If you're not free to go then ask him whether you are under arrest or being investigated for a crime. If the cop says yes to either of those questions, then you ask for an attorney. Just say, "I want an attorney" and nothing more. That's it anyway; you're about to go to jail.

Once again, be polite about it. There's still some chance he'll let you go if he doesn't feel he needs to question you anyway. But remember, if the cop arrests you because you don't want to answer questions that are none of his business, you know that he was going to arrest you anyway.

The same thing goes if he asks permission to search your car. While recent court decisions have broadened a cop's right to search your car without your permission, there are still instances where he needs it. If he asks, do not give your permission. This is essential even if the cop goes ahead and searches your car, because you can get the search thrown out if necessary.

Probably he'll either search it anyway, or he'll arrest you and impound the car and then search it while supposedly taking an inventory.

A Note On Sassing Cops

This is not to give the impression you should stand there meekly and take whatever shit the cops give you. If you feel like it, go ahead and let the cop know you're not going to lick his ass — but do it in a way that lets him know that you know the rules.

For instance, if a cop tells you to do something you don't have to do ("you just go home now" or "keep moving, there's nothing to see here") you can refuse. Even if the cop starts to arrest you, you can read yourself your own rights — "Officer, I haven't done anything wrong but as long as you're going to act like this I know I have the right to remain silent and that I have the right to an attorney. Until I have an attorney I'd prefer to discontinue this conversation." Although knowledge of the law is considered suspect (!) it might give the cop something to think about.

Once you're under arrest, it's a pretty sure thing you're going to jail.

The Smashed Door

This type of encounter is quite different from the calm one described above, and no matter how many times you've seen such arrests live on prime-time T.V., nothing can quite prepare you for it. It is terrifying in the extreme. Your mouth will taste like tin foil and dry up. Your heart will slam itself against your chest and you'll feel like laughing and crying at the same time. You might see your life pass before your eyes. You may feel a deep, deep sense of regret. You might pee your pants.

If the cops come to you by breaking into your house and shouting, there are no subtle ways to influence what happens next. Your initial task is to stay alive or get away. If you don't see a good way to escape immediately, then stay still and don't make any moves. Try to cooperate to some degree — follow their instructions or commands.

Don't look around, don't look at anything. The cops will be interested in those places that seem to interest you. So if you've got your stolen art collection hidden under the bed, don't stare at the bedroom with an alarmed look on your face. Same thing goes for your Hope diamond stashed inside the drywall.

They are going to shout at you and hit you. Generally they will throw you to the ground, cuff you and point guns at your head. Go along with it. You must remember you're dealing with terrified and violent people who are allowed to kill you. And do not say anything at all — especially when they've got guns pointed at you.

If you have children in the house, generally you will be allowed to have the police contact a relative or friend to leave them with. If necessary, press this issue. Knowing your kids are alright is going to help you keep your cool and make you less vulnerable to cop coercion later on. You might consider a plan whereby a friend or relative might be instructed to spirit the kids away should you ever be arrested. In any case, it's too late now to do much about it.

If you have a dog in the house, let the cops know about it. Tell them you've got a dog in the basement or wherever and offer to help secure the dog somewhere for them. Otherwise the cops will likely shoot the dog.

Also, if there are any old people who may be sleeping somewhere, or anyone else at all — TELL THE COPS ABOUT IT. Tell them specifically where what people are so they won't get surprised by anything and pump a few rounds through granny's neck.

Calm Down

Once a certain calm has been restored, identify yourself and then don't say anything else. They're gonna be screaming questions at you ("Where's the drugs!?" "Where's so-and-so!?") but do not answer. After the police have gone this far there is no chance they're going to let you go. This "daring pre-dawn raid" is the culmination of a lot of planning for them. Lots of times they've invited news crews to come along and film such busts. They are not going to treat you nicely — even if the camera's on them! One cop show was sued for showing footage of a very violent arrest cops made on the wrong people!

Once you fall into the hands of the state, innocent or guilty, you lose a lot of "rights." Anything a cop puts in his report is both a public document and immune from action for libel, so it can be republished and otherwise spread around. The film of the raid is considered to be a record of public officials on government business. And of course, cops get filmed all the time beating the shit out of prisoners and get away with it. They don't really care. This should help confirm how far from likely it is that a cop will be prosecuted for anything he or she does!

Once you're in the squad car you may get a prime chance to escape, as sometimes police will just cuff you and shut you up in the car — without locking you in — while they go back to the crime scene.

Now a cuff key hanging around your neck might come in very handy, no? Most handcuffs used by state or local cops are of the same type — and you can buy them, too. One size fits all. If you don't have a cuff key you can order one from the Edge Co. for around eight bucks (1-800-732-9976). Federal cops have got a different kind of key, rounded with flanges like those used on vending machines. "Skeleton" keys for this type of lock are also available. Ex-convicts are often adept at making cuff keys, some that work better than the originals!

Incriminating Evidence

It's best to lose incriminating evidence as quickly as possible. Even just throwing something a few feet from you, or out the window can be helpful. In some jurisdictions fingerprinting isn't standard procedure, so if you toss your baggie full of laetrile into the ditch, and the cops see you do it, there still won't be any real evidence that it ever belonged to you.

Your house may be searched, too. The intensity of a search is very dependent on what the cops think they will find and how badly they want to find something. This is one place you might be able to mitigate the damage early. If cops break in, it may be a good idea to let them find something just so they'll be happy. Cops just want to do their jobs and success is measured in number of arrests that aren't absolutely bogus. So it has happened that cops have shown up at a guy's house with a search warrant for drugs and were simply led to the ounce or half ounce of marijuana the guy had hidden in the closet.

While it may seem ridiculous to lead cops to evidence, in one case it prevented the cops from going any further — and discovering the indoor pot farm this same guy was cultivating in his attic.

On the other hand, if the cops have come specifically looking for your indoor pot operation, no bag of dope will deter them. Still, it's wise to spread things around. If you have a lot of cash, put a chunk of it in the air duct and much more of it flattened out between the boards of stairsteps, or underneath a tile floor. Of course, good cops will look for things like fresh paint or pry marks and if they are serious about finding every thing possible, they will literally tear the walls down. Federal cops, especially, will backhoe your whole yard, dig up your septic tank, drag rivers, anything, if they don't get what they want right away. God forbid they should accuse you of kidnapping, as they will never let up.

The principle here is to satisfy the cop as quickly and with as little evidence as possible. That's why it's not so crazy to let them "have" one or two things. An unregistered gun, a joint, anything that's illegal but not too illegal, is enough to get a good arrest and enough to stop any further search.

In The Squad Car

Please, don't think you'll get away with it by hiding evidence in the cop car on the way to the police station. But sometimes that's your only choice.

If you happen to be arrested with a wallet full of hot checks or a bag of dope or anything else you wish you didn't have on you, you can stuff it down behind the seat. A lot of cops are aware of this trick, though and check this area after they get to the station. It is also possible to do this backwards and score something for free.

That there is dope behind the seats in the backs of cop cars is disturbing since it means either the cop is stupid or it's there to use as "evidence" against whomever they want. A lot of times, drug dogs brought to your car to search for drugs go crazy on the cop's car first.

Better than shoving it down the seat is to drop it on the floor and kick it under the front seat. While they might find it there sooner, it's not as likely they checked there after the last prisoner before you took a ride. And of course, whenever they do find it, you've never seen it before!

The Three Rules of Criminal Law

Deny, deny, deny.

No matter what evidence they have, deny. If they have a videotape of you ripping off the cash register, you deny. Deny no matter what. Confession is crucial to a successful prosecution (more on protecting yourself during prosecution later) so it is important that you just keep saying, "Some other dude did it." Never "come clean." It won't make you feel better; it will send you to jail.

Take a tip from President Nixon and just deny everything.

Now that you've been arrested, you're going to jail (if you don't escape). For more on escape see the relevant parts of this book.

After it's been established that you're on your way to the hoosegow, you must start to assert yourself a bit to the cops. This will not only alert them that you're not an idiot, it will make your sojourn in jail easier, and probably your trial, too.

Ask Questions

At this point it becomes a little more important that you open your mouth. But only to ask some vital questions.

Remember, don't answer any questions, but there are some you should ask. Ask the cops where they're taking you, ask if there is a case number, or any other number associated with your case you need to know. Write this stuff down and give it to your lawyer or some other person you trust.

Ask them if they will allow you to clean up a bit before leaving. Offer to do this in front of them, make it clear you don't want to play games, you just want to shave first. It won't take five minutes. If you've been a good arrestee till this point, they should let you. So take a shower and for God's sake, shave! This is very important.

The Pee Wee Problem

Consider the case of Pee Wee Herman who got caught beating off in public. It wasn't the "crime" that ruined him at all. It was his picture. The Pee Wee Herman we knew was almost sexless and benign. More than anything else the public was shocked by that mug shot. Instead of the harmless man-child, we saw a goateed dog-rapist. There was no doubt, once the mug shot was published, that Pee Wee was beating off in the movie theater and even people inclined to give him a break thought twice. Even people who didn't see anything wrong with beating off in a porno theater were upset. It was the way he looked.

The guy in the picture looked like he was capable of anything.

Pee Wee pleaded to avoid a trial. And good thing, too. There's no doubt the prosecution would have blown up that picture and waved it in front of a jury and they would have sent his ass to the electric chair if possible.

Don't let this happen to you.

One of the first things that happens to you at the police station is they are going to snap a mug shot of you and that is going to become your Official Picture. It's the one the newspapers can slap all over the place without your permission and it's the one the state is going to show to the jury, often to prove what a low-life scum you are even though you've put on a suit for the trial. No matter how slick you look at the trial, the right mugshot can destroy your new image, making you look capable of anything — especially lying.

You've got five minutes to look like a human, so make the most of it.

Be A Good Citizen

Ask to call your lawyer. Then ask the cops to let you call your mother or someone to come feed the dog, pick up the mail, and know your whereabouts. Not only does it make good sense to take care of things like this, it's vitally important that someone on the outside know where to call to see if you're still alive. Telling your mom over the phone that you're being taken away by the cops to such-and-such a jail will also let the cops know you don't intend to just disappear. If there are other people in the house who are not being hauled away, show concern for them. Is granny going to be alright? What about the kids, the dog?

If they've fired a tear-gas canister into the place, there's a very real possibility that your house is on fire. Ask to make sure the house isn't on fire. Ask what you can bring with you. Can you bring a newspaper? Your Bible?

Not only is jail a boring place where reading material would be most welcome, you can use this to your advantage later on in a hearing. How will the cops look if your attorney makes them say in front of a jury how they left your dog to starve and wouldn't even let you bring a Bible or call your mom?

One more thing. Go to the bathroom before you leave. You may already be scared shitless so take advantage of that. You may not get a chance for ten or twelve hours or more. Even then you may find your first chance to take a shit will be in the single toilet serving a cell with 26 guys in it.

You don't want to have to pull your pants down and squat in front of a bunch of pissed-off "tough guys" with something to prove.

One last thing — lock up the house. No need to be burglarized while in jail.

Surrendering

You may be informed by mail or phone that you've got to surrender yourself to some sort of lock-up. In this case, make all the above preparations and more. Remember, you're leaving on an unplanned trip and you might not be back for hours... or years.

Choose your time to surrender well. Don't surrender on a Friday night when all the violent drunks are coming in. One of the best times to go to jail would be mid-morning on Tuesday. On Monday people are grumpy. By Tuesday they've resigned themselves to the work week and will be nicer to you. Also, should something get screwed up, you've got regular working days to sort it out. Friday night jailings mean you probably won't get out till Monday afternoon. A weekday visit during a slow time can mean getting out in a few hours.

Bring your attorney with you to the jail. Often this will expedite things enough so that you won't even have to spend time in a cell. And your attorney's presence will be a reminder that someone is looking out for you. You look far less helpless and less tempting when you have allies.

What To Wear

Don't wear a suit to jail — it's inappropriate and identifies you as a member of a group (guys who wear suits to jail, i.e., morons). It's important not to wear anything that identifies you as a member of any group, not even inadvertently. Wear a red sweatshirt and you may be mistaken for a gang member and get treated accordingly. Cops will be rougher with you and you may end up getting killed in jail by a member of another gang.

Dress inconspicuously and dress for comfort.

Even if you've been arrested from your home late at night in a smashed door incident, you may be able to put on some clothes. If you get that chance, make the best use of it. First, wear shoes with velcro straps instead of laces. That's because they are going to take away your shoelaces once you get to jail, along with your belt or anything else they think is a safety hazard.

Use the "layered look." Jail temperatures are rarely comfortable and change as more people get stuffed into cells or as guards open windows to air the place out, let snow in or whatever. Jails in winter time can get very cold, so wear a couple of T-shirts underneath a flannel shirt. A pair of jeans and thick socks are your best bet and don't forget your underwear!

At the jail they may give you clothes to wear but it still may take them a couple of days to get it together. Besides that, by wearing your own clothes, you can often bring things with you. I know one guy who was taken into custody, booked and thrown in a cell in a Georgia jail without the cops ever detecting the pistol he had in a pocket of his bulky Army coat.

Otherwise, you're going to jail as is. Try to remember this whenever planning for a fun-filled day of law-breaking. You get caught derailing trains while wearing a tutu and you're going to have to wear that in jail and possibly in front of a judge.

Money

Any cash you have on you will help you out initially, as it will be put on account at the jail right away. This will enable you to get smokes, coffee and junk food from the jail commissary more quickly. Otherwise you might have to wait a few days or longer before anybody can get money to you.

Having a lot of cash, however, is not such a good idea. A lot of cash — and that can be just a couple hundred dollars in some cases — is considered to be suspicious and may have even resulted in your arrest. At jail, it may result in you getting a higher-than-normal bail. Besides, you are almost sure to forfeit that money to the state anyway.

On the other hand, getting busted with a lot of money or an expensive car or some other valuable property — while increasing your likelihood of arrest — can save your ass for the same reason. If the cops really like your car (or your money), your lawyer can often get them to agree to drop charges in exchange for your promise not to try to recover your stuff. For more information on this see the section on Asset Forfeiture.

It may also serve to keep your ass out of jail in the first place. More than one person has been shaken down by the cops for his money or drugs and simply let go. The trick is not to look like you have more where that came from.

Sounds like some third-world, fascist, police state, doesn't it? Welcome Home!

Sometimes this extortion works even more simply. The cops will seize your car or take your money and not even bother to arrest you. It is understood, however, that should you complain, you'll soon be arrested and prosecuted.

Either way, if you get the chance to get away by buying your way out, take it! Don't try to "stand up for your rights." It's too late for that now. Doing anything "for the principle of the thing" is foolish at this point. Besides, you're not making any of the rules.

Jail Life

Jails vary quite a bit in quality and there are literally thousands to choose from with new ones being built all the time! Since the prison business thrives on cost over-runs and the like, jails and prisons are likely to be planned by top-flight architects with serious architecture in mind. That means it will be planned for fewer prisoners than it will ever receive. It might have "pods" instead of cellblocks and a cafeteria-style chow hall complete with salad bar. It may also have some great flaws. Graft ensures shoddy workmanship, no matter how good the design. One jail turned out to be nearly useless when prisoners discovered they could simply kick a hole in the cheap materials the builders had used in the walls.

Lots of times jails are in the same building as courtrooms and police stations and other government offices. This can be pretty convenient not only for the authorities, but for the prisoners, too. Once again, there was a case of jail prisoners pushing away part of the ceiling in their cells and then crawling across to the evidence room and nabbing drugs that were kept locked up there.

But don't count on this. Most jails are crowded and filthy. Even a jail that is just a few years old is probably encrusted with filth and grime from all of the people who have been incarcerated there. It stinks. You have to shit in front of people. It's no fun. In even smaller cities, the jails are horrendous. The amount of violence and degradation that occurs there is beyond imagination for most upright, cable-lovin' Americans.

Once you're at the jail, continue to ask questions and don't take anything for granted. If they're moving you along and you see a pile of blankets, ask if you can take one. Or just take it. The nice warden isn't going to bring you one later.

After you get fingerprinted and photographed you may be told to take a piss test. You may refuse it and you should refuse it, even though it may result in higher bail. But if your sample comes up dirty, then the prosecutor is going to use that for higher bail anyway, and use it against you later on, too.

The possibility of a false positive or just plain falsification of the results are far too great to take a pee test. It amounts to answering a question and you must know by now you don't have to, and should not, answer any questions.

How To Behave

More than anything else, jail life is boring. You will probably be segregated with other guys who have similar offenses. This means if you've been arrested for a felony, you'll be in with others arrested for felonies — including murder, etc. The severity of your crime has a lot to do with where you get held. You might be with some pretty rough people.

Being overly macho in an effort to avoid being victimized can backfire. Chances are you'll be seen as a challenge or your act will be seen as a front for your true cowardly feelings. Then you'll end up in a fight. Getting in a fight means you could be seriously injured or have to seriously injure somebody else, which could result in more charges against you. Even so, fighting reflects poorly in the court. So avoid fighting.

But what if the dude is challenging you? This is the moment everyone fears. You're lying on a bench and some guy tells you that's "his" place. What do you do?

No Exit

First, there's no good way out. This is part of the pain and there is no getting out of it. So look at your situation the way we have all along. What do you want? The least possible pain. If, in your estimation, taking on the 300-pound guy who snarls when he talks will bring less pain, then stand up to him and fight. Otherwise, choose your own battles.

Generally you need to appear confident and brave. You may stand your ground for only a moment and then give in, but do it with a glare and be prepared to continue the argument later. You must give the impression that it is just not worth it to fuck with you. So resist anybody's guff with as much as you can, bearing in mind your goal of getting out soon and in good health. If you're only going to be in jail a day or so, don't worry too much about appearing weak in front of anyone. With any luck, you'll never see these guys again.

But, if you can't make bail or are being held for a capital crime, you might not be getting out for months, so obviously the goal is a little different. In that case, mind your own business while being aware, but not involved with, what's going on around you. Don't become indebted to anyone for anything. Not even a pack of potato chips. And you must not allow anyone to try to "punk" you; that is to outright disrespect or take something (anything) from you. If you must fight, fight to win ... it's better to fight and be respected for standing up for yourself (even if you must take a few lumps) than to have to endure being humiliated and pushed around.

Any weakness (like not standing up for yourself) will be taken advantage of and you'll become a target for extortion, sexual assault, and perhaps even having your food taken away. It is undeniably best to avoid trouble, but if it is unavoidable, then stand your ground and rumble with all you've got.

Don't turn to the guards for help. Don't even be too familiar with any of your jailers. Once again, they are not your friends, and if you go to them for help you'll risk a multitude of troubles, the least of which is being labeled a snitch. If you get beaten up in jail, unless you are dying or seriously injured, don't even seek their help — you'll heal on your own. If you must seek medical help, then say you slipped in the shower and never tell who did what! Even if they threaten to send you right back to the same cellblock, you say you don't mind, since all you did was slip in the shower.

Never tell. Prisoners respect such behavior and will leave you alone if you exhibit it. After a few months you'll start to fit into the "flow" of jailhouse living and you'll get used to the foul air, bad food and madness to some degree. By the way, homemade wine (often using a toilet for fermentation) is normally plentiful. So are drugs, but beware of a set-up!

Your Mouth

Don't speak to other prisoners about much at all. And never speak of the specifics of your crime — jails are full of desperate men who will very quickly pick up on anything you say to fabricate a story about how you "told all" to him. And prosecutors are more than happy to play ball with these parasites.

To this end it is best not to reveal any details about even the most mundane parts of your life — that you eat peanut butter sandwiches, have a green cadillac, come from Florida, your wife's name — anything can and will be used against you. It's probably not a bad idea to give misinformation to everyone you talk to in jail. Tell everybody lies and lie about everything. Even though this may be the loneliest time of your life and you'd give anything to take some comfort in another human being's company, realize you can't do that in jail.

Don't write down anything about your crime and don't speak about anything incriminating on the phone. Don't speak of it anywhere or with anyone — even a co-defendant. Cells may be bugged if nothing else.

Fellow Prisoners

Another reason not to talk to other prisoners is that they might just be cops. If the state doesn't have enough evidence to really crucify you, or if you're charged with a horrible crime, they can and do send in undercover cops to gain your confidence. These guys are under no obligation to inform you that they're really cops, or read you your rights.

If they don't succeed in getting a confession out of you, they might also try to set you up for some other crime. Be especially wary of anyone who offers to "fix" your problems because he knows somebody. This is bullshit. Be even more suspicious if someone invites you to commit another crime with him or offers to kill some star witness for you. Desperate though you may be, this is a set-up and if you so much as grunt assent, you're looking at a charge of conspiracy to commit murder or attempted escape or worse!

If you want to escape, do it by yourself or with your co-defendant, and tell nobody about your plans. Even if you discover a source of drugs or do anything else illegal — don't talk about it.

In any event, unless you're being held for a capital crime you probably aren't going to be spending a lot of time here. Unfortunately there's no *Barron's Guide* to jails or prisons, and quality varies widely. Most jails are overcrowded and filthy. Time is usually spent in a day room watching T.V., exercising, gambling, playing cards and/or reading. If you get sick, notify the medical staff or the guard who "runs the pill lines" (brings the medications around) and see if you can see the doctor. Emergency problems can be brought to any guard's attention and, if necessary, other prisoners are willing to help bring attention by banging on bars, screaming and generally making a fuss throughout the whole cellblock.

If your request for sick call is not honored within a week, write the sheriff and/or file a grievance about being denied medical care and that will usually remedy the situation quickly.

Bail

In many jurisdictions, bail has been set for all the various crimes and a formula has been developed to figure out what yours will be. There might even be a chart on the wall in the jail explaining the various amounts of bail for whatever crime, which can either be increased or decreased depending on a number of factors.

How the cops feel about you is a factor. Whether you're a first offender is a factor. Whether you waved a gun around is a factor.

The best is to be let off "on your own recognizance." This is often not hard to get if your offense is minor and you have a job or have some kind of family member waiting to take you home. The jails are always chock full and "O.R." (as it's called) is a distinct advantage, so try for it.

Otherwise, bail may be set right there, or you may be held without bail pending a hearing before a judge. If you've been arrested for some particularly heinous crimes there may be no bail in the world for you. First degree murder, for example, is not usually a bailable offense.

Once you know what your bail is (and your attorney should have at least tried to have it lowered for you), you've either got to put up that amount or else get a bail bondsman to do it. Bail bondsmen charge

10% of the whole bail, a fee which is not refundable. So if your bail is $1,000, then you give him $100 and kiss it goodbye.

Strangely enough, some states have decided to get into the bail game themselves charging just 1% of the bail money, which fee also is not refundable. It may behoove you to see if your state is participating in this scheme. Yes, it does seem a little shady that the state sets bail and then sells you bail insurance, but this should just remind you of the nature of the criminal justice system.

Jumping Bail

If you jump bail, you burn the person who posted it for you. If that's a bail bondsman, he's likely to come after you, and so will bounty hunters (especially if the bail is high). If it's your grandma who put up her house as collateral, don't forget to pay her back if you ever win the lottery while you're on the lam for the rest of your life. If it's the state, you can bet they will never forget and if they catch you, they'll make you pay and pay and pay. Probably you'll get time.

The Interrogation

There is really only one overriding rule for resisting cop interrogation, whether at the time of arrest, at the police station or in jail. Keep your mouth shut. Never, never, ever say a single thing without your lawyer's permission. Don't ever discuss anything AT ALL with the cops. Pretend that everything you say will be heard as "I did it" — because that's how it will be interpreted if you do anything except ask for your attorney.

Still, cops are very good at this aspect of their jobs. Confessions mean everything to them and to prosecutors. With a confession, the case is closed and the cop has won. In truth, cops couldn't care less if you're "back on the street in five minutes." Their only job is to arrest you and make it stick long enough for you to be indicted. Confessing or incriminating yourself just makes it that much easier. Remember, if the police really had evidence against you, they wouldn't even be talking to you.

But they do talk to you. In fact one of their games is to pretend that they do have evidence against you and your confession is mere formality. Don't fall for it.

Don't fall for the "Good Cop, Bad Cop" routine, where one cop seems be barely able to restrain himself from killing you and the other appears to offer some relief. As well-known as this game is, it still works — even on cops!

Resisting interrogation is not easy. It's very difficult. But you must resist, since a fuck-up here will just drag you that much deeper into the machine. As we shall see later, an unsuccessful interrogation is the kiss of death for many prosecutors who've got plenty of easier cases to try.

So, steel your mind and say nothing. If the psychological pressure gets to you, just babble a cartoon theme song or something. But never talk. Ever. Not even if they bring in a video tape which shows you clearly committing some crime. In that case, assume you are hallucinating and shut up.

It is possible that you will get an even more rigorous interrogation, especially if you get picked up by the FBI or the Secret Service or some other federal police agency, including the Army. In this case they may resort to physical torture, which, it is generally accepted, is not resistible in the end. Enough pain will make anyone confess to anything at all. This is one of the reasons torture is not more routine, as it requires a skilled torturer who can tell when a subject has stopped telling the "truth" and has just started to make up stuff to save himself from pain.

The subject of resisting interrogation is one you should study further if you believe you may have to confront it one day. In that case, please refer to the Appendix for further reading.

2
Trial

Arraignment

Once you've been taken to jail, it's time for your arraignment, when formal charges are brought against you in front of a judge of some kind, often called a magistrate.

Normally you have a right to this hearing within 24 hours of your arrest, but as a practical matter, getting arrested on the weekend can extend the wait two or three days. It also makes a lot of difference where you're arrested. Big cities run court sessions all night long.

The important thing is that you have an attorney now. Ideally, you've already lined one up for just such an occasion, but we'll assume for the moment you didn't.

You Need A Lawyer

First, you must have a criminal lawyer. You can forget your family's tax and estate attorney — if he takes the case you're sure to go to jail. However, he may be able to recommend a criminal lawyer for you. But, it cannot be stressed enough that you need a lawyer who is a criminal defense attorney and nothing else. Criminal law and civil law are very different from one another in procedure, methods of proof, and everything else. And the stakes are so much higher in criminal court that you cannot have half-assed representation.

It almost goes without saying that it's far easier to pick a lawyer and prepare your defense from outside jail. Although it's possible to do it all from behind bars, you're subject to all kinds of obstacles and you are essentially helpless. In this case you can improve your lot by having a trusted person on the outside help you out. Best of all is a family member or a close friend who has nothing to do with the case.

You must insist that the lawyer come visit you immediately. Even if you are fortunate enough to have trusted people on the outside to do this for you, you need to see your lawyer in person. That way you'll know for sure what's going on and won't feel so helpless.

Criminal lawyers are only about 3% of all the lawyers out there and of those few, probably 80% are either just scraping by or worse. Even the ones making a living off it are not doing too well. Yes, there are high-priced, high-profile defense lawyers out there, but you won't get that guy. Luckily, there really are a lot of good court-appointed defense attorneys. However, in your present circumstance you'll have to choose quickly from little information.

There is one important thing to keep in mind when hiring a lawyer that may seem obvious but bears noting. Make fucking sure YOU are the one paying the lawyer. If your pal Luigi says he's taking pity on you and has decided to provide you with his own personal lawyer and will pick up the tab, you must refuse. First, because even the lawyer knows it's not truly ethical, and mainly because if the lawyer is paid by Luigi, that's who he works for, and not you. You and your pal Luigi might have very different ideas about what would be a successful outcome to your case.

Your lawyer should be just that — *your* lawyer.

How To Pick A Lawyer

Look for experience and training. Contrary to popular belief, state-provided attorneys from the public defender's office are generally the best you can get. They have often got many times the training the prosecutor has, and have clocked more hours in court. Your prosecutor could easily be a total rookie since this is one of the first jobs law school grads can get and the pay is not too bad.

Your attorney may have even worked for the prosecutor's office at one time. This can be good, but it is not necessary at all, and you should watch it if the guy harps too much on his knowledge of the system gained from being a prosecutor. If he was a prosecutor for very long at all, his mind is likely warped by the experience. He'll make you think he's working hard for you, but his sympathies are elsewhere and his concern for you is low.

The public defender is local and so also knows the judges, secretaries and other people who can really do things. He may even intimidate the prosecutor by virtue of just being around so long and knowing everybody. He doesn't need to be high-priced or famous, either — in fact, revving up the profile of your case may be the last thing you want. A good, local boy with solid experience getting people out of the hands of the criminal justice system is what you need.

So your public defender's office is a fine place to look for a lawyer. He's only got one real problem — he's impoverished. Unlike the prosecutor, the state pays him less, gives him more work and fewer hours to do it in, which does tend to overburden him. But all public defenders are up for grabs as private attorneys as well, and many depend on this outside income for their bread and butter.

Don't scrimp on your lawyer. Your life may literally depend on this guy, and what he does in the next few days can make the difference between going home that night or heading for the state penitentiary in a bus with wire mesh over the windows. He'll tell you his price and you pay it if you can at all afford it.

But don't get carried away. There's no point in offering him any kind of bonus for anything. Telling him you'll double his price if he wins may tempt him to throw caution to the wind and go for broke. Remember, in the end, if he loses, you go to jail.

· But if you're broke you still have a right to an attorney, and he or she will be coming from the public defender's office anyway. In fact, it might be to your advantage to go indigent — that way the lawyer's free.

So you get someone who's connected with the PD's office. If you can, try for a younger guy. A young guy has more energy to devote to your case, is less jaded and less likely to take an assembly line attitude toward his work. He's more likely to fight. It's also easier to assess him.

Older guys can all seem pretty confident due to their jadedness. It may also be easier to relate to a younger guy.

By the way, it is NOT necessary to tell him everything. Until you get a better feel for the dude, be careful what you say to him. He may sell you out, or even make it worse for you.

There are two schools of thought on the matter. Lawyers will tell you never to lie to your attorney and to reveal as much information as possible so they'll have the most to work with. And they've got a valid point. On the other hand, you may accidentally skew things by telling things that don't really matter and give him the wrong impression. You might piss him off or otherwise negatively impress him, so he'll be happy to pocket your money and send your ass to prison. It's true that whatever you tell your lawyer is privileged information and they're not supposed to reveal it. But don't rely on this.

Unfortunately, there's no good rule here. It's generally a bad idea to lie or withhold information. But at this point details are not as crucial. At this point you need that lawyer to get these charges dropped and show you a way out of the machine.

Perhaps the most important thing to keep in mind about your attorney is that YOU bear the responsibility for your defense. You must govern and control the relationship. Have your lawyer provide you with copies of all paperwork he files, and brief you and keep you informed on all meetings or contacts he might make relating to your case. If you're stuck in jail, this is even more important. If you're in jail you must write and call your lawyer constantly, not to harass him, but simply to show you have an active interest. If you don't have an active interest in your case, you can bet he won't.

Like everybody else, attorneys are lazy. It's to their advantage to hit you up for their fee, then get you to plead, thereby saving them the work of defending you. They may even use some of the scare tactics used by police to make you think you're facing a worse situation than you really are, so that the plea bargain they offer seems like a better deal.

More on pleading later.

Make sure your lawyer demonstrates his interest; he should at least come visit you before your hearing, for instance. You must feel satisfied that he or she is doing their best for you. If not, fire them and get another attorney — you have a right to do this at any time. At the same time, don't become a nagging asshole — you must work as a team.

The Hearing

Once you've been caught in the maw of the machine, it is important to mitigate early to minimize the damage. Your preliminary hearing is the place to do this and your lawyer is the best one to do it.

Have him thoroughly check all police work connected to the case — the warrant, the circumstances surrounding your arrest, everything. Cops, in their eagerness to make a bust, often break the law. Prosecutors include things that have no bearing on your case just to make you look worse. In federal cases, things like that are explicitly used to determine how bad your offense is. For federal purposes the "abuse of trust" bumps you up on the offense chart. A doctor who sells drugs is worse than a plumber who does the same. So having shit thrown at you like that can be seriously damaging.

But errors like that must be discovered and corrected quickly. All too often a guy doesn't realize there was some major flaw in the state's case against him until it's discovered years later by a jail-house lawyer or his own research. And, while the discovery may very well lead to your release, you may end up sitting in prison for five years when you could have walked on the first day!

Worse, to combat the "problem" of appeals and other forms of due process, some states are adopting laws making it increasingly difficult to introduce "new" evidence once a verdict has been initially reached.

Your preliminary hearing is the place where a lot of pain can be avoided. Take advantage of it. This is the first place the charges "stick" or not.

The preliminary hearing is where the judge gets to hear the prosecutor explain what crimes you've committed and has to decide whether you can be prosecuted for them or not.

Here's where your lawyer should get a lot of the charges against you dropped — especially those crimes you did not commit. To get you prosecuted, the state must show that you've fulfilled certain "elements" of a particular crime. For instance, one of the elements of burglary is that you must have been inside the house. Now, if the cops got you outside as you were lurking around, that's not enough to charge you with burglary, since you don't meet an essential element of the crime.

The Prosecutor

If there is any one monster in the machine who is truly out to screw you, it is the prosecutor. It is his or her job to crucify you. The prosecutor does not care at all about you or fairness or anything else. All the most vile elements of a policeman and a politician are concentrated in him. This person is your archest and most dangerous enemy, and has the power to legally inflict all kinds of sadistic shit on you with a few strokes of a pen. This is no exaggeration. Even the meanest judge might bother to listen to your side, but never the prosecutor. He or she will stop at nothing to ensure the worst for you. Prosecutors hang out with cops and are likely to participate in the corruption and abominations those guys commit. Small-town prosecutors might even mosey down to the jailhouse to taunt you or participate in beating you. They are truly merciless.

Treat the prosecutor as if he were a bird of prey. Many animals avoid being eaten by predators by looking skinny and bad-tasting; follow their lead. Do your best to look skinny and bad-tasting. Do not antagonize this person. Act humble as hell in his presence — act fucking scared. You shouldn't have any trouble doing this because, rest assured, he wants and intends to hurt you. His effectiveness and his livelihood are measured by the number of people he hurts and the severity of the pain he inflicts.

All you want to do, or can do, at this moment is minimize that pain.

A Three-Pronged Fork

At the time of arraignment the prosecutor can do one of three things: forgo prosecution; prosecute you; or refer it to a grand jury. The grand jury is often used when a prosecutor, for some political reason, cannot avoid prosecuting a case he would prefer to ignore. A good example is when a cop kills an innocent person, or the city's richest citizen gets caught doing some crime. Then he can take it to the grand jury and get THEM to issue the indictment and blame the prosecution on them.

In fact, it is true that a prosecutor could "get a grand jury to indict a ham sandwich" if he wanted to. The "trial" is held in secret. All evidence is picked by the prosecutor and all the witnesses are compelled to testify (no Fifth Amendment here).

Originally, the grand jury was supposed to be a way for the citizenry to protect itself against some maniac prosecutor by making sure that a jury of your peers thought you were a scumbag, first. This system has been perverted into a game in which a group of "solid citizens" routinely OK a prosecutor's wishes while acting as his scapegoat should he fail to win the case.

The Mind Of The Prosecutor

Prosecutors are interested in two things: a confession and evidence. If you've followed instructions so far, you haven't given anything like a confession. Now it's up to your lawyer to suppress any evidence. Sometimes you can do a good enough job of convincing the prosecutor that there isn't much evidence that you'll look skinny and bad-tasting, and he'll spit you out right there and just forgo the prosecution. Same goes if the prosecutor feels he's gotten ahold of some prey that may fight back. Your lawyer, your behavior, your looks, everything must convey to him that you will not go cleanly or easily to trial, that you will fight him every step of the way and that you are capable of it.

Let him know you'll be filing motions right and left, that even if he gets a conviction, you're the type who can get it overturned. You are but one of scores of guys the prosecutor is going to screw that day, so it's not so hard to convince him there are easier meals than you.

Another important thing to communicate to him is that your case may well have "overtones," be they racial, sexual or anything else. Remember how that cop wouldn't let you bring your Bible to jail? Cops screwing up at the scene — especially by shooting uninvolved people, or setting a house on fire with tear gas canisters — are a good thing to have on your side. It looks horrible in court. More than once the state has prosecuted a man and ended up defending itself (and losing) against a hellacious lawsuit because of cop misbehavior.

Sometimes prosecutors are stupid enough to charge you with a crime you clearly didn't commit and the charge is thrown out by the judge. But prosecutors never just charge you with one thing. Along with any main charge will be things like "disorderly conduct," "resisting arrest" and the like, and it is a virtual certainty that the judge will find enough *prima facie* evidence to allow you to be charged with something.

Your attorney's first duty is to bust down as many charges as possible, so that you face the least of them. You absolutely need a lawyer to do this. Legal training is necessary since it is essentially the charge, and not you, that is on trial before the court. That means that your "alibi" isn't of much use here. Alibis and the like are what is known as a "positive defense" and that's not considered here. All that counts now is that the charges look proper. To defend you, your lawyer must show that your case doesn't fit the legal definitions of the charge.

There are lots of ways to do this but your lawyer is the one to do it. This is your first chance to cross-examine the cops and the whole thing should be recorded by a court reporter, or at the very least recorded on tape. Cops can easily change their testimony later on and you may need to refute them.

If your lawyer can't get a charge thrown out, he might at least offer mitigating evidence to show "diminished capacity" and get the prosecutor to drop the charge. Drunkenness, emotional states, and other circumstances can serve as a "defense" here to get the charge "decriminalized" (instead of attempted burglary, you can become a glue-sniffer in need of treatment).

You can have felonies reduced to misdemeanors, misdemeanors to infractions. The main thing is to whittle the charges down to something simple, something a jury can understand, something you can defend against. Far better to be charged with theft than criminal conversion — the latter may not make much sense to the jury. Same thing goes for any other "gobbledygook" kind of crime like "stalking" or "conspiracy" or doing anything "with intent." Vague charges are easier to prove since nobody's quite sure what the hell it is. In any event, you're probably not getting out of all the charges, so it's on to the next step.

Before The Trial

First offense.

If your attorney is successful in reducing the number of charges against you he may also be able to get you into one of the many "pre-trial diversion" programs in operation all over the country. These programs vary in details but basically are a way to speed things up and lighten the case load and they all work in a similar way.

In exchange for you doing some sort of penance thing, the state will agree not to press charges, and, if you stay cool for six months or a year after that, they'll even expunge the whole thing from your record. This last part is important because it means you'll have a clean record the next time you get popped and you'll be afforded all the benefits any other "first-timer" gets. In this way it's possible to get nailed for two or three crimes before anybody starts to notice. It's not always automatic, though, so don't forget to apply for the expungement later on — you never want this charge to show up in front of a judge again. Too many guys are doing "enhanced sentences" because they blew off cleaning up their records and got years of time for being habitual or career criminals, when they could have been treated like a first-offender.

Being a first-time offender is really important. Judges are often very lenient, and so are prosecutors. The next most important thing is to have a job. If you don't have a job when you get arrested, make sure you have one by the time you get to this hearing. It's more important than being married, having kids, or any of that other "responsible citizen" shit.

If your lawyer can argue that the local economy might be slightly disrupted by your being sent to jail, he has an effective tool. Other things at his disposal might be the fact that you've already spent a couple of days in jail because of this, that certain people are dependent on you ... but mainly you have a job. That says you are accepted by society and there's a good chance you won't act up again.

So the judge will make you go to an alcohol-treatment program or perform some community service, and you twist your necktie and thank him profusely. Then get the hell out of there, do your stint in the county dog pound, clean up your record and stay free.

The Plea

If you end up having to go to trial your lawyer will be able to file for "discovery" and you'll get a look at just what the state has against you. You can start to assess what your chances would be at a trial. Now is the time to consider coming clean with your attorney and also to assess him. If he doesn't seem competent, then request another.

The plea bargain is what keeps the courts going at all. Without them, the "justice system" would jam up in one day. There is no way that each person charged with a crime in the U.S. could have even one minute of court time if the majority of people accused of something by the state didn't agree on a "plea bargain." In exchange for a reduced punishment the accused agrees to help the state save money and time on due process.

That way the prosecutor gets to chalk up another in the "win" column and you don't suffer as much. Even if you are innocent, a plea bargain is something to consider — especially if it keeps you out of jail. And that — not justice — is the goal here. If you are guilty and you feel the state has got you cold, then consider a plea bargain even more seriously. It could make a difference of years in a cage!

The plea offer comes from the prosecutor (often transmitted to you through your own lawyer) and reflects just how strong he or she thinks the case against you is. If they have a lot of evidence and witnesses, they may offer only a token amount of time off a sentence in exchange for a guilty plea. If it's weak, you'll see that, too, in the form of a much better deal.

Typically, the state will take their list of charges — robbing a store can be broken into robbery, a weapons charge of some kind, confinement (for each person in the store), fleeing the scene, resisting arrest, etc. — which together could send you away for a hundred years, and offer to let you plead guilty to just one charge and take whatever punishment that entails.

You can counter-offer, too, and once you come to an agreement on what you'll plead guilty to and the punishment, then you go play the scenario in front of the judge. However, the judge is not bound by the agreement and is free to sentence you however he wants. In practice, the judge normally goes along.

Mitigating And Aggravating Circumstances

Whether you should take the offer or not depends heavily on your exact situation. Too many factors are involved to give general advice here — (everything counts) — whether you're in a rural or urban situation, your race, your ties to the community, even the temperature; all make a difference. In most cases, if you're facing two years or less, you can expect to serve that time at a local jail. If it's longer than that, you'll be sent to a prison in another part of the state where conditions may be worse. Thus, if a prosecutor offers 30 months, it may be worth it to counter with an offer for 22, so you can stay in town. Oftentimes the prosecutor can make sure you get sent to a particular prison or jail, and that could influence your decision.

Other things to consider are some of the things used to "enhance" your sentence. Typically these "aggravating circumstances" are doing things like using a gun in your crime, doing it near a school or park, introducing co-conspirators, selling dope to minors and so on. Many of these are statutory, but you and your lawyer must decide if they pose a real threat. For instance, "use" of a gun. Just having a gun in the glove compartment while you sell drugs is "use" of a gun during a crime. If you trade a gun for contraband or accept one as payment, that's "use." As more and more oppressive laws aimed at disarming the population come into effect, more permutations of this will be possible.

For instance, if you have grandpa's old shotgun in the basement while you sell untaxed cigarettes upstairs, that probably won't stand up as "use" of a gun (although they'll threaten you with it). But if it's an AK-47, or has a banana clip or just looks like one of those guns the media is demonizing, it may very well stick. Sometimes you'll be threatened with a gun enhancement if someone connected to you in the crime had a gun at home. This is another case where it probably won't stick — at least as of this writing.

Another thing you MUST see before you decide to plead is any kind of pre-sentence report or investigation. This thing will typically be full of errors that must be corrected. In federal cases you have a right to review this report for at least 10 days before sentencing. If your lawyer doesn't get around to showing it to you, then you object to it at sentencing and demand your ten days — not a minute less. They might try to give you a half-hour in the hallway to check it over, but that's not enough. You are entitled to 10 days and you will get it if you insist.

More on these pre-sentence reports later.

Plea-bargaining is something you should take under reasoned advisement with your attorney, something you must think about very carefully. Don't jump on anything, even if you're pressed. Especially don't allow anyone — not even your own lawyer — to scare you by telling you you're facing a possible hundred years if you get convicted of the whole string of charges and if you have to serve all the sentences consecutively. Although that's possible in theory, it isn't likely. If the only "bargain" you get offered is to have a few minor charges dropped, that's not much of a bargain. You have to weigh the offer against what is likely to happen, not what could conceivably happen. Think carefully.

Think carefully because the carrot of a lighter sentence is balanced by an enormous stick. Sometimes, like the police, the prosecutor will threaten to hit you with charges he or she knows aren't true but will get you a lifetime in prison if he succeeds. It is a sick game indeed, especially if you're innocent.

Failing to plead and forcing the state to go to trial means they will come down very hard on you if you lose. You'll be sure to get the maximum punishment possible if you are found guilty, so keep this in mind if your attorney urges you to "go for it" and "we can beat it." If he's wrong, it's you who goes to prison; he just goes home with an even bigger wad of money than he would have made from a plea-bargain.

On the other hand, it's not a guaranteed win for the state, and, should the trial go in your favor, you go free.

As discussed above, your lawyer may be biased in favor of pleading just to avoid the work involved. The best protection against this is to know what the likely sentence really is. Sometimes, as in federal cases, this is pretty easy. Since 1987, all federal penalties have been standardized by Congress. Judges are bound by these guidelines and have almost no latitude to go above or below them. Figuring out your sentence is as easy for you as it is for the judge. A system of points assigned for every aspect of your crime determines your sentence and even the type of prison you'll go to. A lot of states have mandatory sentence laws, too (especially for drug crimes).

All of the sentencing guidelines are published and publicly available. Anyone with more than two weeks of law school can find them for you. Your criminal lawyer will be able to interpret them for you.

One thing to remember is that indeterminate sentences such as 2 to 12 years mean very little if there is a mandatory 10 years for a crime. If the minimum mandatory sentence is 5 years, then you're really looking at 5-12. A plea that gets you 8 might not be so good then. If you're a first-time offender or have other mitigating circumstances, then you'll probably only get five anyway. And be especially wary if the prosecutor offers you a "deal" wherein he lowers the minimum in an indeterminate sentence plea. Maybe instead of 5-8 he says he'll ask for 0-10. Remember, the sentence minimums remain in effect. If the minimum is

5, then 5 is the least you can get. To be a legitimate offer, he's got to offer a reduction in the maximum sentence.

A plea should get you something. You're agreeing to trade some of your freedom to save the state money and hassle. Get something for it.

"Rolling Over"

Just as at the police station, the prosecutor may also give you the chance to snitch on your friends or to otherwise help them go after someone else. Like any other offer, it will reflect just how badly they want you to snitch, though your reward will be commensurate with the quality of information you give and there's no guarantee of anything once you've sold out.

Don't do it. If you testify against someone or help the police entrap somebody else, your days are numbered. Once you have allowed yourself to be used by the police/prosecutor, they will throw you to the wolves. There's a strong possibility that the police will say your information was of no use and hit you for the maximum anyway. If there is a mandatory sentence in effect and they don't lower the charges against you, there's no way for them to deal with you, regardless.

Informing or otherwise helping the prosecutor is a stupid idea. Even if they really could get you a better deal, you don't want to become an informer. Informers are the most hated people in the world. Even the cops think informers are scum; prisoners absolutely loathe snitches. If you're in prison there will be nothing you can do to prevent being raped, brutalized, tortured and killed. Even if you are set free you will not sleep soundly ever again.

Once identified as a snitch, there is no way to get out of it. No apology can ever be sufficient, and you will be hunted down. "Protective Custody" in prison won't do you a bit of good. Even the most sophisticated "witness relocation programs" might buy you a little time but cannot protect you forever.

Don't become a snitch and don't listen to anyone who advises you to do it.

On The Other Hand

Every criminal defendant has something to sell — he may not be aware of it, but he does. You may not have to turn in your buddies, you may have only to furnish some specific information the prosecutor is interested in and which you won't end up betraying anyone with. Maybe you know, just by living in the neighborhood, about certain things the cops wish they knew. What are some of the signals used by drug dealers in your neighborhood? How, exactly, is a certain scam being run?

The state might also want you to help them in some other way. Perhaps they want you to take the rap for some other crime that's not as bad but, for some reason, they want it disposed of. In any event, if you hang out with criminal elements, you may very well be in a position to trade information for freedom.

Some prosecutors don't care much about quality. They want five names. So you give them five names of your enemies. Some prosecutors may even let you back out on the street where you can go find some people (perhaps rivals?) to turn in. Some are not this dumb.

They say everyone has his price, and prosecutors will tell you that sooner or later everybody, but everybody, informs. Some people agree to inform and then back out later when they realize what they're doing. Some crack right away. The trick is to give the cops information they already have, is no good, or will not make you a hunted man.

If you've been nailed in some kind of high-level embezzling scheme, the prosecutor (and the company) may ask that you reveal your methods in exchange for less-harsh treatment. Hell, you might happen to know the layout of a certain house in your neighborhood. You might be able to identify somebody you don't even know.

Then again, you might have some property they want. You could easily trade this for something. This can happen either as asset forfeiture (described below) or just by revealing where you have hidden something valuable.

But once again, selling out a live human being who has a chance to get at you, ever, is a stupid idea. By the way, this is one reason Luigi has so kindly provided you with his slick attorney — part of his job is to see that you don't make any deals involving Luigi's hide.

You Need Rehabilitating

Just as we saw at the preliminary hearing, other things that can help minimize chances of incarceration or reduce your sentence even if found guilty at a trial are having a job, distinguished military record, well-known surname, family support, community or church support, no criminal past and, of course, having drug or drinking problems.

The beauty of being a dope fiend or a drunk is that the court gets to sentence you to rehabilitation instead of prison. It is far better to be convicted of being a low-down drunk who steals than to do time for burglary. Make sure your lawyer considers this angle — to blame your crime on drugs or drink and then let the state "save" you.

Of course there is also "remorse" if you plead or get found guilty. If you can't get off by presenting yourself as a human garbage can, then at least let the world know how sorry you are. Abase yourself. Never smirk at anyone, do not laugh at your trial.

Don't smirk or laugh if you're pleading innocent, either. And for God's sake, don't cry. Crying is remorse and that means you're guilty. Just express worry and shock.

And never, never, never "throw yourself on the mercy of the court."

The Bribe

At this point, it is also possible to pay off various people and make a deal to essentially buy your way out of the machine. This doesn't have to be in the form of a classic bribe, where a judge gets a plain envelope of cash and you get acquitted. In reality, these deals are hard to initiate and extremely dangerous for all concerned. Although your lawyer may be able to set this up for you, this type of pay-off is restricted to Mafia types who also have the time-tested threat of assassination, etc., to back them up.

And if your case is highly publicized, a judge would be committing political suicide to "go easy" on you.

If your case is not so public, you may be able to swing one of those deals where the policemens' orphan fund suddenly gets a large anonymous donation. Or the prosecutor's nephew lucks into a brand new job at the company you own, or any of a thousand permutations on this type of "understanding." Needless to say, you have to be rich to pull this off.

Luckily (in a perverse way), the bribe as we all know and love it has been institutionalized to allow even the "little guy" the chance to pay a guard and scramble free. Especially for smaller offenses, prosecutors will openly solicit funds for the policemens' orphan fund in exchange for not prosecuting you. But this kind of thing is confined to smaller offenses. If the crime is more serious, however, there is still a chance to buy your way out of it. This type of bribery is known as "asset forfeiture" and it has bought thousands of people their freedom.

Asset Forfeiture

Asset forfeiture has made it possible for a guy to buy freedom by striking an unwritten agreement with the prosecutor that he will not complain when the state takes possession of some or all of his property, if the state promises to reduce the penalty or even forget the whole thing. In practical terms, the seized property need not be too expensive at all — a car or a computer might be plenty enough. Sometimes a used CB radio is sufficient! Anything with resale value can be fenced to the state in exchange for a lighter sentence.

This is possible because it is the police departments themselves that benefit directly from seized goods. So does the prosecutor. Sometimes a prosecutor's entire income is dependent on the amount he can squeeze out of people the state has accused of a crime, so you can guess where he is coming from! As an example, there is one large city in the U.S. where a single attorney handles all of the asset forfeiture cases on behalf of that city's county and eleven other surrounding counties in the state. This is a busy man. He is also a very rich man, since he is paid a percentage of the assets he is able to seize for the state.

Yes, it's raw extortion, but it must be handled carefully nonetheless. Offer your custom van too early and the prosecutor may even act offended that you'd think of such a thing. Offer too late, and... it's too late. Here is yet another reason to have a local criminal defense attorney who knows each prosecutor's quirks.

Asset forfeiture makes it possible for the state to take away your property as long as they allege it was somehow, even tenuously, involved with a crime. You have the option to fight for it and get it back, but it's a losing proposition. Even if the case is dismissed, they can keep your property. Even if you successfully sue to retrieve it, you have to pay the storage bills.

Sometimes the grab can be even easier. Cops in airports especially are always sniffing around for someone with lots of cash on them. One of the first cases of a state airport mugging was the case of Roger Liukkonen in Ft. Lauderdale, Florida. When cops there relieved him of nearly $15,000 in cash (not arresting him either) he sued to get it back, spending $7,000 on lawyer's fees. In the end he had to settle for a portion of it, as further litigation would have been even more draining.

Even in the heartland, police stopped a woman in the Indianapolis airport, took $35,000 in cash they found on her and didn't even bother to make an arrest.

Since 1980, some fundamental and startling changes have been made in state law that have made property seizure from criminal suspects a true billion-dollar industry. Under a host of laws purporting to strip gangsters of their ill-gotten gains, a suspect can now be deprived on the spot of his money, house, car, bass boat or anything else he owns if a cop has "probable cause" to believe the assets were gained or used or intended to be used in the commission of a crime.

That crime can range from premeditated murder to possession of rolling papers. From kidnapping to jaywalking. If you do it twice it can be deemed "racketeering," subjecting even more property to forfeiture.

Furthermore, the state does not need to convict, charge, or even arrest a suspect to seize his assets. To get them back, the suspect has to prove to the satisfaction of a court that the money or assets were not gained or used illegally, or if they were, that he had no knowledge of it. This kind of "convictionless" seizure came into vogue at a federal level in the early eighties and has now been mimicked on a local level by nearly every state in the country. The public outcry for a "War on Drugs" and now the more generalized "War on Crime" (currently focusing on guns) has made these laws quite popular with prosecutors.

It's popular because the money and goods seized are funneled back to the police departments, making a bonanza out of law enforcement. Prosecutors also like the law because it shifts the burden of proof to the suspect, or to any third party with an interest in the property, so it is easier to keep seized assets.

Forfeiture laws represent little more than a money grab that results from the erosion and elimination of a citizen's right to due process, the Fifth Amendment's protection against self-incrimination, and the Fourth Amendment's protection against unreasonable search and seizure. Spouses of criminal suspects now find themselves suddenly penniless and homeless. Roommates or business partners lose everything they have invested jointly with a criminal suspect. Theoretically, every resident in a condominium complex could lose his property if just one resident is suspected of criminal behavior. Suspected — not arrested or convicted.

Yes, it flies in the face of our supposed "innocent until proven guilty" ethos. After all, due process can be difficult.

The broad language of the laws has allowed police to confiscate an entire video store by alleging an "obscene" tape has been rented there. The store is then out of business and the owners deprived of a livelihood.

Being accused of a misdemeanor can ruin you as the state plunders its own citizens. You don't have to be a crime kingpin; you don't even have to do anything wrong!

Even the American Civil Liberties Union, which has railed against the federal RICO laws as heinous beyond description, has itself been seduced by the power of these laws. Using the criminal version of the RICO statute, it has sought prosecution of abortion protesters who block abortion clinics, charging them with "a pattern of racketeering."

The state can confiscate a suspect's money and property based on mere suspicion. An informant's anonymous tip is enough to launch an extensive investigation resulting in permanent confiscation of property, even if the case is thrown out of court or the defendant is acquitted of the crime.

Yes, it's unconstitutional to deprive someone of life, liberty or property without due process, but this nit-picking point is taken care of by a legal doctrine known as "relation back" which says that property instantly reverts to the state once it's been used for illegal purposes. This view changes the proceedings from criminal to civil, leading to an Alice-in-Wonderland world where the thing is guilty of the crime.

You'll see cases such as the State of Arizona versus a 1965 Mustang convertible, or State of Arizona versus $25,000 cash.

The state uses the laws as a *de facto* form of punishment. The state essentially allows defendants to buy their way out of prison time, or use the laws as a way to levy fines without even going to trial.

Surveillance

Because of this supermarket spree the cops have developed, they have put more and more effort into getting people to spy on each other. You may find yourself entangled in the justice system simply because somebody got pissed off at you and phoned in a "hot tip."

So the cops get a hot tip that you're doing something wrong that'll subject you to forfeiture. Then they can request a mail cover and have the post office photocopy your mail. They can find out where you bank and they can find out if you own property. If you divert your mail to somebody else, they'll just search *their* mail and they will find you and watch you and follow you around — all on an anonymous tip.

Now what ends up happening is, when you start watching a perfectly honest citizen long enough and hard enough, you'll start to develop probable cause for search warrants. Then you can get financial search warrants, and you can go into people's bank records and go inside safety deposit boxes and all kinds of stuff, and that person never knows. You can't find out about it unless you write away to the government under the Freedom of Information Act and request your records.

The kicker? The federal government is the only one subject to the FOIA, and if the stuff's under seal, the court won't tell you it exists. That means that the federal magistrate has said that you're the target of an investigation, and in order to permit the government to conduct its investigation they won't tell you you're under investigation. If anybody in the government told you, they'd get in the deepest darkest trouble they've ever been in in their lives.

As an investigation progresses, it gains momentum and has to justify itself. Any investigation done out of malice is abuse of process and therefore illegal, but by the time a target of an investigation finds out about it, it's too late. And once probable cause has been developed for a criminal violation there is nothing to stop the investigation from intensifying.

They can bring you in front of a grand jury where you're not entitled to a lawyer, and question the hell out of you, and if you answer the first question then you can't even take the Fifth. It's dreadful.

They could put you through a wringer you could not withstand — "accidentally."

State and federal legislatures have consistently strengthened and broadened these laws, extending the amount of time the state can hold a seized asset before going to court, and eliminating rules that forced the police to sell much of the seized property. Now the state has three years to use whatever it seizes. Then it can sell it. Just in case you were ever wondering how you got this far into the machine.

Probation

After the trial, should you be found guilty, you get one last crack at saving yourself some pain. Between the trial and sentencing, you will be confronted with a probation officer or some other similar court employee who will interview you. From this interview, he'll compile a recommendation (sometimes called a "presentence report") that the judge is supposed to read before you get sentenced.

Your probation officer can undo much of the damage done so far. He can also make things a lot worse for you, so you must lay it on thick and heavy during the interview. Should there be anything incorrect or improper in the report, make sure your attorney objects to it as soon as possible — you have the right to be sentenced based on correct and accurate information! Jail behavior is also considered at the sentencing — same goes for the old military record, community ties, and remorse song and dance. They may also have negative things such as hearsay from enemies. Make sure to correct that.

Even though you're sure to go to jail or prison by now, the sentencing is where it's made official and it all gets spelled out. It is a crucial time, to say the least. Most of the time a judge will go by the recommendation he receives. In fact, it is the probation officer, not the judge, who has the most say-so over what happens to you.

That means you may be able to have a new trial right then and there!

It's important not to get caught lying to the probation officer, but in no way should you tell "the truth." When speaking of your criminal history, make sure to separate yourself from the past as much as possible, and in every possible way you must downplay any gains you made from crime. The parole officer doesn't want to hear any tales of the good life you lived while robbing houses or selling laetrile. In fact, a good citizen "going bad" can be written down as a reason to give you an even harsher sentence. It's not a legal reason to enhance your sentence, but you'd better get it out of there before the judge sees it! If your lawyer won't do it, then write him a letter insisting that he do it, and send it to him certified mail. Documentation is everything in an appeal!

If possible, suggest that you were forced into the crime, that you never would have done this except for some circumstances beyond your control. In fact, everything about your crime has to be beyond your control. If you come off looking like a key underworld figure, you'll be punished for it. If possible, suggest that someone made you do it by threatening you into it. Otherwise, maybe you did your crime because your baby was starving or for some other misguided but noble reason.

It isn't necessarily a bad idea to blame part of the crime on being drunk or otherwise intoxicated. But do not blame it on chronic drinking or drug-taking. This not only will not be seen as an excuse, it may make it worse. Certainly, from then on you'll be known as an alcoholic or drug addict and be less likely to get parole or other breaks. It may also subject you to a narrower range of prison conditions if you get pegged as a "problem" prisoner even before you're locked up!

But own up to the crime. Let the judge know you know you're ultimately responsible for what you do. In federal law, this acceptance of responsibility is even codified, providing for a two-level reduction in offense classification. So you are the only one responsible and you are sorry. You are very sorry. Your words must drip with remorse. This is by far the most important thing. You must be sorry for what you did. You did it and you're sorry.

Sometimes a judge will go bananas over something, ignore the presentence report and, out of sheer abuse of power, send you away for an extra twenty years. Even if you're able to get the sentence overturned, you're looking at a hell of a lot of work and not much chance of success.

A good example of someone who pissed off a judge is Jim Bakker, who got more than 40 years for crimes anyone else wouldn't get ten for. Luckily, the judge blew it by taking a moment to lecture the "disgraced preacher" on how much he considered Bakker an asshole. Bakker's lawyers were able to use that to get him released about thirty years early — but not until after Bakker had served a lot of time with that sentence hanging over his head.

So plenty still rests in the judge's hands (unless he is constrained by sentencing guidelines). He can make you serve sentences concurrently or one after the other. He can find you a habitual criminal and invoke "sentence enhancements" that will add long years to your time — or maybe give you life! He can sentence you to "flat time" in which you must do a fixed sentence or he can give you an "indeterminate sentence," the famous 2 to 25 years. The good thing about such a sentence is that it may be possible (it varies from state to state) to start going before the parole board after only two years (unless there is a mandatory minimum).

On the other hand you may have to do the whole 25 years.

You may not even get a chance to get out early, since the judge could just pick a number between two and 25 and give you that as "flat time."

It's impossible to recommend which state is "better" than another for any given crime here, as there are so many variations between states, and laws are changed and enforced so capriciously. In general, however, for drug crimes, the state penalties are lighter than the federal penalties.

Of course, most crimes are still state crimes, and you won't have much choice between state or federal prosecution. But don't worry, the federal government is taking long strides to usurp this, and soon every crime can be a federal crime!

The sentencing laws in states vary quite a lot, and the same crime in one state that gets you 4-8 years may bring you a flat 20 in another. Some states don't have parole at all but do have what's called "good time," meaning you get a certain amount of time off your sentence for each day you "behave." In general, it is wiser to reduce the range of sentencing — 10 years flat is better than 2-25. Sure, you might get out earlier with the second sentence, but probably not. It is more probable that you'll get the whole 25!

None of these sentencing schemes contain even the tiniest loophole, and all of them have some horrifying drawbacks. For instance, any low-paid guard can destroy your chances of "good time," thus effectively taking control of your sentence once you're in prison. All he has to do is accuse you of any kind of infraction and you will be punished immediately. Along with whatever punishment you get (the hole, for instance) comes a reduction in time class and more time on the end of your sentence.

But you're not incarcerated yet. Right now you still have a chance at that fun carnival known as "the trial"! Put on your party hat!

The Trial

Your first decision on a trial is whether you want to be tried by a judge or a jury. Common wisdom says you should go before a judge if you've got the facts, and before a jury if not. This is true to a certain extent, but when your life is at stake it's wise to consider the matter more deeply.

A lot of prisoners have 13½ tattooed on their hands or arms, which stands for 12 jurors, one judge and a half-assed chance. At a jury trial you have only to convince one person you're innocent to get a hung jury. At that point the state has to try you again or let you go. If you get another hung jury, the likelihood is that they'll just drop the charges (but keep the threat of re-arrest over your head) to avoid wasting more time and money and looking like fools. Or else the prosecutor may offer a really sweet plea bargain.

On the other hand, if you go for a bench trial (judge), he or she is going to come to a decision. From there that person decides how to punish you. Your fate rests entirely with a person you have never met before. The only thing good about a bench trial is that if you're found guilty the state may not be as pissed off at you (since bench trials are cheaper), and give you less time. It also may be to your advantage to go before a judge if you're charged with a crime that is repugnant to the community.

That means if you're charged with pimping, go to a judge, but if it's assault and you can show how the whole thing resulted from some kind of on-going feud, a jury is more inclined to show mercy. Child abuse — judge, wife-beating — jury, etc.

Statistically, for all crimes, juries are 50% more likely to acquit than a judge. You have a better chance at getting off with a jury. If you want a knee-jerk choice, go with the jury.

In any case, it's time to re-evaluate your lawyer. For a trial you want a litigator; that is, someone whose job includes a lot of actual arguing in court. Large law firms often employ guys whose only job is to argue the case in court. They don't do a lot of research or develop a case as much as they use their skills in persuasion. Litigators are guys who can think on their feet, make quick and accurate guesses as to where the prosecutor is going, and stay aware of their surroundings. They should also be able to discredit or otherwise destroy any of the state's evidence against you, or any of their witnesses.

Your defense lawyer is likely to also be a litigator, but make sure of this. It may be that he has a partner who does the litigating just because he's better at it. This is one place where TV bullshit has some truth to it. Perry Mason did a lot for his clients with his courtroom antics. Your lawyer can too.

It is a colossal mistake to have an inexperienced litigator argue on your behalf.

Mike Tyson (once incarcerated for rape) made this mistake. Tyson not only used a lawyer inexperienced in criminal law, he also chose a man who had not argued a case in public for years. The importance of having a good litigator was made doubly clear in the Tyson case when the state of Indiana hired a private outside attorney to argue the government's case, even though they had recourse to any number of ruthless and experienced litigators in the prosecutor's office. They wanted to make sure they won, and they did.

Even though juries are "safer" than judges, they are not automatically sympathetic. Bear in mind that a jury trial means you will be watched by 12 of the squarest people within a hundred miles. These are the people who couldn't think of a reason to avoid jury duty. These people have demonstrated to the satisfaction of at least two opposing lawyers and a judge that they have no real opinions on anything. They are people who have an abiding respect for authority, dullards at best, reactionaries at worst. They are going to watch you for the slightest sign that you did it. They believe everything the judge says and they are going to either punish you or set you free on essentially the same basis as they vote for politicians.

And damn near anything can convict you. You must not swagger, nor must you trudge along. Though you have the right to remain silent that is generally interpreted as a sign of guilt. And when you testify, you will lose if your testimony isn't seamless or if the prosecutor is able to rattle you.

Be humble. Don't assume you can sit there scowling or digging in your nose while your lawyer "fixes" everything. Guys like John Gotti (Mr. Swagger) or Mike Tyson (Mr. Smug) are examples of bad jury performances.

Jury Tax

There is, really and truly, a "jury tax"; that is, you will get a harsher sentence if you make the state go through a jury trial to find you guilty. This is not written down anywhere and nobody will admit to it publicly. But sometimes this jury tax is so explicit, judges have been known to call defense attorneys to their chambers just before the first day of a trial and threaten to give the defendant twice as much time if he is found guilty.

Even after you get "taxed" by the judge, you may find that the sheriff or the warden or whoever is in charge of your carcass while incarcerated simply has a policy of not honoring "good time" accrued by defendants convicted by a jury. Some authorities are not even shy about writing this down as a reason to keep you in jail when they could let you go. Nope, it's not constitutional, but it'll be a long tough fight to win — if you can prove your case. The pressure here is immense to say the least.

Don't Look Back

Whatever avenue you take, especially in a jury trial, you've got to stick with it and never look back. This will take balls, as there are going to be lots of moments you'll feel like breaking down. But don't. You must play this out to the end.

Behave yourself in court, and project a positive attitude that a jury can admire or identify with. You must appear to be "the good guy" and at the same time you must appear to be "just like them." People don't send themselves to jail, after all.

This may explain why John Gotti was able to win all his acquittals in the past with his super-confident, expensively tailored-suit look. Maybe the jury just drooled to be like him. Maybe the last time he seemed too self-assured.

It's true, for instance, that it's a real bitch to go after a movie star in either a criminal or civil suit because of the jury's natural "star-worshipping" tendencies. Burl Ives could be videotaped sodomizing a boy's choir and he'd walk. That's another good reason to bring on the charismatic character witnesses — if you can link yourself with beloved personalities they will compare you favorably against the prosecution. Church and business figures are good people to have speak up on your behalf.

Needless to say, keep your cool. Never stand up and declare this or that witness a liar. Don't fall asleep, fart, groan or do anything but pay attention. If your crime includes a coroner describing the badly mangled body of a young girl found by the riverside, don't get too emotional, just show some disgust like any right-thinking person would. Once again, concern and worry are your only valid emotions.

It's generally a good idea to testify on your own behalf. Silence means you're guilty to a jury and it's hard to imagine any good reason to stay away from the stand. Even if you have a voice like fingernails on a chalkboard or a whopping case of Tourette's syndrome, the jury wants to hear you say, "I didn't do it." You get up there and say it. The prosecutor might make you look horrible, but that's his job; yours is to get the hell out of there with an acquittal.

Mistrial

A guy in Florida realized his jury trial was not going the way he wanted it to and decided it was a lost cause. His only hope, he thought, was to get a mistrial and start from scratch.

To this end, he simply waited for the correct moment, then punched his own lawyer in the mouth as hard as he could. The lawyer was knocked out of his chair and there was blood and commotion. The judge screamed at the guy that he was still going to sentence him, etc., etc., but our hero sat there passively. He knew the trial was no good. It was a mistrial and he was entitled to another one.

Normally there's not a lot of advantage in a mistrial, as it almost always results in another trial at which the same judge is likely to start influencing things more than usual — either to make sure that doesn't happen again or to punish you if you pull a stunt like the one mentioned above. Still, it is a legitimate delaying tactic and can be considered. Getting a mistrial, like filing a cascade of motions, objecting to everything and countersuing, buys more time. In some cases this may be your best hope — it is possible to outwait the prosecution. As time passes the state may become more amenable to a deal, your case may fade from public view. Key witnesses against you may get sick of constantly having to come long distances to re-testify. Hell, key witnesses may even die!

There is something to be said for dragging out your case as long as possible, though you should make sure you have the funds to do this. You may need quite a lot. After all, the state has almost unlimited resources. Matching them dollar for dollar could be a losing proposition.

The Jury

There is a lot of speculation on who is good to have on a jury. Blacks are supposedly less willing to vote guilty. So are "liberals," bikers, and others who may have suffered at the hands of authority.

Young women are thought to be some of the harshest, most reactionary of people to have judging you. So are crime victims, military guys, and cops.

In reality, the jury is a very local phenomenon and although there is a degree of truth to some of the above beliefs, they might vary a lot from community to community. Once again, this is why you must have a local attorney, who knows all the neighborhoods and probable backgrounds of potential jurors. He or she should ask each a bunch of questions designed to figure out what sort of prejudices each one actually has.

Each attorney is allowed to disqualify a certain number of jurors without stating any reason at all. Use these when something in your gut says, "no." All other exclusions must be for a reason the judge agrees with.

FIJA

The Fully Informed Jury Amendment (or Association) (FIJA) is one break you still have left to get out of the machine without being ground into a fine mush. It has gained in popularity over the years and scares the hell out of cops.

It is the jury's right to find a defendant "not guilty" of breaking a law if the jury does not believe the law itself is just. Judges will tell you differently, but it is true. Even if the defendant clearly has done all the things the prosecution alleges, the jury can still vote to acquit if they think the circumstances warrant it, or if they simply disagree with the law.

"Jury Nullification," as it is known, is the jury's right and duty to judge the facts of a case as well as the law itself. It is the reason a little more than 50% of the people accused of violating Prohibition laws were set free. Juries simply did not agree that a man who had alcohol should go to prison.

Time and again authorities (including judges) at every level of government have sought to prevent the dissemination of Jury Power literature — even in those states where the "fully informed jury" information is required as part of the instructions the judge is supposed to read to the jury.

In states where the Fully Informed Jury Amendment has become law, the intent of the law is effectively thwarted by the judge himself.

Typically he, or she, will rant on and on about how the jury must take a narrow view of the facts, how they must not form opinions based on anything but that what they have heard in the trial. They also very often tell them they are required to follow the judge's instructions only. Then, to comply with the law, they mumble a legalistic phrase at the end of their two-hour harangue that, translated, means — "oh, by the way, half of what I just told you isn't true. The jury is not only empowered, but required to judge the law itself in each case."

Judges have also repeatedly refused to allow attorneys to speak of the jury's right to consult their own consciences when considering whether or not someone is "guilty" of a "crime." They are frequently unaware of the severity of the punishment the accused is facing and are even told at times "don't worry, this guy is going to get off light," when that's not true.

In short, judicial tampering with the jury is what leads jury members to express regret right after a trial, saying things like "I didn't think he did anything wrong and I (or we) didn't want to find him guilty, but the judge said..."

If you are on a jury and you feel the slightest pang about a guilty sentence, you must go in the direction of mercy. In fact, that's the only direction a jury can take — juries can only show mercy, not heap on punishment. There's a reason for that and it's called justice.

Seems a lot of judges are unfamiliar with the process and concept.

If you are accused of a crime you believe most of your peers think is stupid, or you believe they would acquit you for no other reason than the punishment is out of line with the "crime," you need to inform your jury of this right.

This is not always easy to do.

It will be easier to inform the jury of its true powers if you plan ahead by contacting FIJA beforehand. If you must wait till the shit hits the fan, you should still call them at 1-800-TEL-JURY. With their help it may be possible to "contaminate" potential jurors with this information.

Escape

Escape is an option at any point along the path to the electric chair, although it becomes progressively more difficult to escape as you are sucked into the machine. Your first chance to bug out is while you're being arrested or pursued. Then of course you can jump bail. Once you get to prison it becomes a lot harder to get away but it can be done! There has even been one successful escape from death row!

But that guy, like so many others, was eventually apprehended.

The fact is, most people who attempt to escape prison succeed in their initial escape. Then most escapees are caught fairly quickly, usually within a couple of miles of the prison. This is mainly due to incredible stupidity. A man will spend every waking moment scheming and fine-tuning a brilliant escape, only to be apprehended the next morning at his girlfriend's house! Sometimes guys are nailed just sort of hiding out in nearby scrub land, clueless as to what to do with their new-found freedom.

Because there are many methods of escape, I will leave it up to the individual to figure out when and how to effect an escape. But keep in mind that once you wriggle away from The Man, you still exist and will have to be somewhere. If you don't want to go back to prison (and get more time for the escape attempt) you must vow to run far and fast and never, never come back.

In *Steal This Book*, Abbie Hoffman wrote of the isolation of going underground and stressed the determination one must have to remain at large. Then he proved his own theories a few years later when he disappeared. He returned to the public eye at a time of his own choosing — a time when his political enemies were gone and the public had nearly forgotten him. Abbie is an object lesson to anyone who decides to make a break. You must disappear completely and probably forever.

One reasonable thing to do is hide out in an area where authorities are not likely to look for you and, if they did, wouldn't have much chance of finding you. If you can go it alone in the mountains, then head for the hills. Not only will you be left alone for the most part but you may even gain the upper hand over your pursuers should they continue to chase you. The main thing is to get away from the cops' turf and into a place where you have an advantage.

Pick a place you like. Like the place you pick. The famous French escape-artist portrayed in the book *Papillon* was able to get away from some of the most bestial conditions anyone could imagine in South America's French Guiana. At one point he lived for years with an Indian tribe where he ate well, slept well, had at least two wives and gained the respect of the tribe.

There in the jungle and on the beach, he was invulnerable. No French authority would dare hunt for him in such hostile territory, and the Indians would help defend him. Eventually he left this idyllic life for stupid reasons (revenge, mainly) and ended up back in hell.

If you find yourself in such a situation, don't be a fool. Don't come back. Instead stretch out on the beach and enjoy your freedom. Leave the old world behind, physically and mentally.

Remember what happened to Butch Cassidy and the Sundance Kid ... although they had the right idea by going overseas.

Extradition

Hiding in a foreign country has the immediate advantage of very clearly leaving the jurisdiction of your pursuers. In fact, if they find out you're somewhere in Bolivia, they might just forget you. Depending on the charge, it may simply not be worth it to try to catch you. If they only know you left the country, then, hell, they probably will forget you. Roman Polanski has nicely evaded a nasty bout of incarceration by this method and you can too. Just be prepared.

A couple of terms to become familiar with before hitting the road are "extradition" and "the doctrine of comity."

Extradition treaties are agreements countries have to send back each other's bad guys even if they don't personally have a beef with them.

You are shit out of luck for the most part in these countries. These treaties are common and can even form a daisy chain that will keep you visiting prisons around the globe for centuries. Some of the nicest countries have these treaties, so, in the words of the U.S. Customs, it's best to "Know before you go."

But don't give up hope. Lots of places are quite loath to enforce U.S. policies they don't agree with and will drag their feet when tracking you down. This is how U.S. draft-dodgers and army deserters managed to stay in Canada for so long. In fact, by running away, and staying away long enough, they were eventually granted amnesty while their stateside counterparts went to jail or war. The Canadian government didn't agree with the U.S. war in Vietnam and one way they showed it was by leaving the draft-dodgers alone. Same thing happened in Sweden.

Cubans running to America get practically automatic citizenship no matter what they did in Cuba. For a long time, Algeria was home to Eldridge Cleaver because they perceived him as a political ally. Another example is Germany, which doesn't like to export criminals facing the death penalty although they'll play along with just about anything else. Israel has protected Jews just because they're Jews. Brazil won't extradite the father of a Brazilian baby. The key to choosing which country to run to is to find one with a common interest.

Comity is basically an agreement between all countries to allow each other's judges all around the world to slap each other on the back and tell each other how right they are. So, even in a country with no explicit extradition treaty, you may find yourself sent home to jail. An example of this doctrine of comity at work is seen in airline hijackings. Air hijacking is considered a crime all over the world and normally hijackers get sent back to the States (or to prison right there) even if the country is at odds with the United States. About the only exception to this is, once again, Cubans coming to the States.

Wherever you go it is important to be on your best behavior. This is where Butch and Sundance slipped up and went down in a hail of Bolivian bullets. Keep a low profile to increase your chances of living a carefree life. This means not committing any more crimes while you're there. It means asking not what that country can do for you, but what you can do for that country.

Bring lots of money. Everybody is friendlier, the richer you are. Bank robbers often have plenty of coin and thus can induce banana republics, which might otherwise throw them out like a dirty diaper, to harbor them in comfort — at least until the money runs out. Becoming a citizen can help, too. But you're still at the mercy of politics, as former Nazis have found out from time to time even after being protected for decades. And think of the spies who defected to the Soviet Union. Where are they now?

Again, in running overseas, choose your destination carefully and don't count on luxury once you get there, even if the country hates the United States. Just check out all those hijackers from the 1960s who fled to Cuba only to remain there to this day cranking out license plates.

3
Prison

Here's what it all comes down to. You've been chased, caught, and trussed up. Charged, tried and found guilty. You've made all the deals you can for now. You're going to the big house.

Your legal options aren't played out yet, by any means (there are post-conviction appeals, for instance; pardons and the like), but that doesn't matter much now — you're on your way to the most feared place on earth. Barring the truly extraordinary, you're also going to be there for awhile; years probably, maybe the rest of your life.

You might be going to federal prison or you might be going to a state prison. It's also possible to be convicted in federal court and go to a state prison anyway.

As with all the other choke points in the machine, there are many ways for you to go. No matter how deeply you get sucked into the machine this remains true all the way up to death row where, in some states, you still get to choose the method you will be killed by.

But we'll get to that later. For now, it's plain old "controlled custody."

The Frying Pan

Your prison experience nearly always starts out in a local jail, where you may have spent the past few weeks or months already, awaiting your trial if you couldn't get out on bail. In jail you've experienced what it's like to be isolated from society, thrown into a cesspool of filth and violence, cut off from all civilization.

Those visits you did get were through a thick piece of dirty plexiglass — which only accentuated your isolation. Same goes for the rough treatment at the hands of guards and the rushed, don't-give-a-shit attitude of your public defender as you tried to get him to plead down the charges against you, to get you the fuck out of here! If you've spent much time at all in a city jail, you will, by now, already know something of overwhelming loneliness, desperation and fear.

In big cities you're certain to have witnessed some violence as bad as anything on TV. Maybe as bad as you can imagine. In some places, more than three out of four prisoners are violently attacked each year. Prison is bad. Big-city jails are as bad or worse than prison.

Now that you've been sentenced it gets worse. How much worse it gets depends partly on the severity or nature of your crime, the space available in the prison system, and a number of other factors including the judge's mood that particular minute he banged the gavel. It also has a lot to do with people who are your true judges. The person who files a pre-sentence recommendation, for instance.

It's true there are some federal minimum-security prisons that are not horrible (though none ever reach "country club" status). The other side of the spectrum is lopsided, with many enormous complexes of old and foul buildings where life is like something from a post-apocalyptic holocaust. The windows are small and covered with bird shit, there are wire mesh and bars everywhere. It smells like a bus-station urinal. The light is dim. The thick, stinking air is full of tuberculosis and typhoid.

On cellblock tiers, trash can pile up waist-high. There's garbage everywhere; some of the walls are smeared with feces. Prisoners gang up in packs and roam through the burned-out, decaying prison at will, surviving directly off the weakness and misery of others. In places like these the guards are at best of no value to the prisoner. At worst, they form one of the meanest and best-equipped gangs.

It has happened, and *still* happens, that a prisoner is tossed into one of these subterranean worlds and quite literally forgotten. In nearly every state prison, at least one or two people have been found who had finished their sentences years ago. No one had noticed. Or if someone noticed, they didn't bother to release them.

State prisons above minimum security are much more like this terror-filled world of violence and disease than the "country club" prisons. Prison conditions probably reached their nadir in the mid to late '70s, when prisoners were able to run amok and murder, and suicide was a very frequent occurrence (every couple of weeks in any given prison). Order has not been restored, if it was ever there to begin with.

Getting Prepared

If your sentence is much more than a year, you're going to prison but you will probably remain in jail for awhile — maybe months — before getting transferred to the pen. This is due to the intense over-crowding that exists in nearly all prisons. Use this time to get ready for your trip. (You can avoid some of the following hell by getting a self-surrender clause in any plea agreement you make. You still go to prison, you just don't get cattle-prodded around for a few months first. Oh, and if you surrender, don't try to bring your teddy bear, and for sure not your legal papers. The demons at the gates of hell will only let you in with the clothes on your back and maybe a cheap watch.)

Ask around, especially with the older cons who have done time in various state joints, to find answers to some of the nuts-and-bolts questions about a particular prison. Can you keep your clothes? Watch? How many cartons of cigarettes can you have? Find out what things are allowed or not allowed and then get friends or family to drop off a package of items for you to take with you. Most jails allow this. You won't be given access to them while you're in the jail, but they'll store them for you until you're transported to prison. Often, things like a good watch, a pair of "street" jeans (i.e., jeans that fit), colored/hooded sweatsuits and the like will come in handy, as you may not be able to get them once in prison. And all of these things (as well as hard-core pornography) are as good as cash behind the walls.

If dope of any kind is your thing, stash away all you can in jail — it's cheaper than in prison, and can also be sold in prison. You might also grab all the cash ("green") money you can, as that, too, is forbidden in the penitentiary. Be as creative as possible in concealing these items.

Most "new" cosmetic items (packaged soap, deodorant, etc.) are not too carefully inspected when you go through intake at prison, and they're almost always allowed when coming from jails.

But you probably aren't going to jail right away anyway. Your first stop is a facility known as a "reception" or "diagnostic" center, or some similar euphemism, where you will be confined for weeks or months. These places are much worse than jail for a variety of reasons.

The Reception Center

Sounds cozy doesn't it? Almost like they'll be serving coffee and donuts... Wrong.

The reception center is where you will be made fully aware that you are a captive. For one thing, you will probably be shipped there in chains — literally multiple chains. Your hands are cuffed, your feet are chained together, and another chain links you and a number of other prisoners together in a line. Heads of prisoners are automatically lowered as they get paraded out on the streets between jail and court, jail and the reception center.

Soon after arrival at the reception center you will have your hair cut off. To further rob you of dignity, you'll also be stripped naked and your clothes will be taken away. Sometimes you'll get the option of sending them home, sometimes the clothes will go to charity. Then you disappear into this clump of humanity and get herded around with all the other men, shuffling around in response to orders barked by guards. You'll be made to bend over and spread your ass cheeks so a guard can peer or even poke a finger up there.

The degradation is complete and deliberate. Here you're going to learn to swallow all your anger, embarrassment and pride. Resistance is futile. The guards will meet the slightest resistance with a serious beating.

You'll be herded through a fast shower, sprayed with insecticide and given an ill-fitting uniform and your number. And you're asked the "50 questions" about whom to call in case of an emergency, etc. Your personal property will be inventoried and divided into three classes: what you can keep, what you can have once you arrive at prison, and what you can't have again, ever.

Generally you'll be allowed to keep cigarettes, coffee, unopened boxes of cookies and your wedding band. When asked how much your watch is worth, make sure you say less than $30 or they'll take it.

Reception Centers are often stuffed beyond simple overcrowding. There will be at least three men to a cell (designed for one). The rest will be on cots or mattresses in the halls and recreation rooms (which can get gruesome, as we'll see). As the men locked up in here go crazy and start to give vent to their hatred, they take it out on each other. Men sleeping along the range beneath tiers of cells are sometimes pissed on from above. The whole place is a din of screeching and yelling. You may have to stay here for months and there are generally no visits for the first month, if ever. Supposedly you're only here temporarily.

There is also no hope. The next step is prison. Very few people are freed from the Reception Center. This place is pretty deep into the gullet of hell — you've already passed the mouth long ago. This is part of what makes the Reception Center so awful — the realization that you are about to be cut off from the rest of the human race. Really, it's more the realization that you already are.

Ostensibly the Reception Center is to give the prisoner some "orientation" about prison life while at the same time the state determines which facility would be the best for the individual. In reality this process has been abandoned long ago, and although you'll be asked the 50 questions and make a quick visit to the "nut doctor," you're going to the first place that has an opening. Stil, you can look forward to a cursory physical and dental examination, and you'll talk briefly with a counselor who will try to assess you for proper placement.

As stated before, which prison you're headed for is already pretty much determined by the crime you've been convicted of, but other things that will affect your ultimate destination are length of sentence, conduct in jail, and willingness to cooperate with the various tests they will give you, such as an I.Q. test.

If you're looking at a long sentence, there is a theory that suggests you be as uncooperative as possible — refuse all tests and tell them you don't care where you go. You're going to a horrible prison anyway and this will generally get you out of the Reception Center quicker. But if you've got a small bit, you might opt to take the tests and play along with all their games, including sitting around this hell-hole for months on end. That way you might end up in a work camp or minimum-security prison.

Usually there is very little chance for jobs or schooling or anything else in the Center, though as soon as you get there it's a good idea to ask to work on the kitchen crew or clean-up crew ("range-runners" or "detail-men"). This gives you access to more places and things, more mobility and chances to hustle. After all, lots of people at the Reception Center still require certain "necessities" (maybe now more than ever) and there are people able to provide these necessities. You can become a conduit for these items. Range-runners are normally out and about all day, sweeping and mopping the tiers, bringing messages and paperwork to and from prison administrators, so they naturally act as middle-men for such transactions.

Do not trust anyone with any of your stuff at the Reception Center. One typical scam is for a guy to promise to provide you with something and "be right back" only to disappear. If this happens to you and you do see this guy again, don't hesitate to beat his ass, even though this may result in going to the "hole" and/or immediate shipment to a segregation unit (another word for the "hole," anyway) at a maximum security prison. Prison is not the place to develop any "bad habits" — like allowing people to "beat" or "play" you — and the Reception Center is no place to start!

You also shouldn't let your business be known if you happen to have dope or green money, or even so much as a bag of Fritos, as you'll end up with 101 "friends," or worse, become a target for all sorts of petty games. Or you may get told on and punished by the authorities. Just as in jail, don't try to be too friendly with anyone and don't try to act tough — these are both signs of weakness in prison. You don't need anyone's help at the Reception Center — the state will provide you with clothes, shoes and hygiene supplies.

The Reception Center is where you are severed once and for all from society. The intensity of hate and fear and sadness is palpable. A letter from your girlfriend or wife can perhaps give a ray of hope here. But probably, no letter will come and its absence will be devastating. The world is bleak and horrid. This is where you'll hear men crying, and where you will see (and get) absolutely no compassion for your situation. Guys who start to crack, to cry for instance, will only be taunted by the others. You are practicing for prison now. You are becoming a con and leaving the free world behind. You are a "fish" being tossed into a scum pond, and you are lower than any pest. Society hates you. It's enough not to hate yourself.

As a new fish you sink or swim. Some guys sink right here. And sinking means death or worse, so make the best of it. Toughen up under the strain and endure this with all your might. Try to keep your mind busy so it won't turn on you. Don't seek comfort in others, because the rest of the fish are just as beaten as you and won't be able to withstand your bleating. Besides, it's not fair to further burden a guy who's in the same shit as you.

That's the way it is in prison, too. The stress of incarceration is so great that it is almost impossible to offer much of a shoulder for anyone to cry on without losing it completely. Prisoners stay away from people who thus jeopardize their sanity. If you can't get it through your head that you're in prison now and life as you knew it is over, your fellow prisoners will help make it clear. The guards will make it clear. Denial is fruitless. You are no exception. You've got to "do your own time."

One day they'll come to your cell and tell you to "pack up"... it's time to go to prison!

For most guys the idea of going to prison, by now, seems like a relief, and they leap at the chance to go even deeper into hell.

Arrival In Prison

Although every prison is different in many respects — some may have a dominating "political" culture, others are more divided along racial lines, etc. — this won't be apparent to the fish. The fish might not have the slightest clue as to what's going on in prison, where the culture is as alien as the most far-off foreign country.

After a ride on a converted school bus with steel mesh over the windows and, once again, chains dragging along the floor, you get to prison. By this time you will have heard every story about the place. On the bus you may have heard a few more from returning cons. Depending on the state, you may have been on the bus for hours on a hard wooden bench-seat. In the wintertime it's cold, in summer it's hot. More than likely the prison will be in a rural area, set off the highway and surrounded by open fields. That means you'll get a look at it miles before you get there.

There will be chain-link cyclone fencing with razor-wire coiled atop it. There may be a "no-man's" zone some 30 feet wide on the other side of it, closed in by another fence topped with razor-wire. The area might be covered with gravel and patrolled by attack dogs.

The prison itself is guaranteed to have watchtowers. The older the prison, the more like a medieval castle it will seem. High walls with small, narrow windows (or no windows at all), gun turrets in the corners and fences everywhere. To get to the back of a prison, where the fish are usually let off, the bus may pass through two or three of these fences, the last one made of steel or iron and built like a Venetian blind in thick slats. The heavy steel gate grinds open and shut behind the bus and it's time to get off.

This is where the fish get thrown into the tank. There are groups of inmates standing around or looking out through windows up above. It is quite normal for the new guys to be so scared their teeth chatter and they shake uncontrollably.

Prisons can vary a lot, again, but normally this is where you'll get back whatever stuff it is you left when you were checked into the Reception Center. They'll also give each prisoner whatever little amenities the state issues its human possessions. A bar of soap, some prison jeans and prison shirt, a razor, toothbrush and toothpaste. Some prisons even give prisoners their mattresses right there and you'll have to carry it with you wherever you go from now on. Some groups of prisoners will come up to you and tell you they're from such and such a club or group and they're here to help you.

The bitch of it is, some of them will be telling the truth. In any prison there are groups of cons who have taken it upon themselves to help in the transition. Some of the older guys might "baby-sit" a new guy for the first week or so, steering him through some of the bureaucracy, showing how to get things done, what to do and not do. But this is not considered to be a fun task. It's enough to be a prisoner yourself without having to take care of someone else. The prison is supposedly going to give you some orientation, too, but as you found out in the Reception Center, that's not going to have much bearing on reality.

Usually you'll be herded off to a dingy cell block or dormitory where you will be given a rule-book, fill out a list of visitors from your immediate family, and asked about where you want to work (or rather, told what's available and asked which you prefer). They'll inquire about your education. If you don't have a high-school education you'll probably be assigned to G.E.D. classes or Adult Basic Education (A.B.E.). You may get a chance to learn a vocational trade. But prisons are overcrowded and job opportunities, such as they are, are slim. While in orientation you'll be closely watched by the guards, but mostly you'll be checked out by the other cons as "fresh meat" or new fish.

The Fire

If you are at all young and "pretty" you can expect taunting from the very beginning. As a new fish, you might be separated from the general population at first during orientation, but very soon you will be thrown in with the "mainline" (general) population and you're going to hear, "Hey, baby, you're gonna be mine," etc. You may be assigned a cell (which is more secure and private) or a dorm. Some prisons are all dorms, so you'll have no choice. You could be put into a makeshift dormitory converted from "rec" rooms and filled with triple-high steel bunk-beds. The "bathroom" will be a row of seatless toilets with no stalls. It might just be one toilet. You're going to be taking a shit in front of everybody.

In fact, once you arrive in a cell block or dorm, you will be a popular attraction — people will look into your cell, hang out in front of it checking you out (and what material things you have) and stopping by out of the blue to strike up idle conversations.

"What's your name?," "How much time you got?," "Where are you from?" etc. You're being felt out and sized up. You're in the jungle and you are potential prey. Some of these guys are just curious and some are predators. You might live with these fellows for the rest of your life.

U.S. prisons are full of some of the rudest, most violent and savage people on earth. They live by an ethic that is absolutely alien to anything in the outside world. In reality, there is nothing you can do to prepare yourself adequately for what is to follow, just as there's no real preparation for war or any other extreme, life-or-death situation. In fact, war is perhaps the closest thing to prison. They are both maddeningly boring stretches of time punctuated by sheer terror.

Of course, the predominant fear of all fish is rape and the prospect of homosexual advances — brutal homosexual advances.

Prison Rape

Of all the fears men have about prison, this is the worst. Loss of liberty, eating bad food, loneliness, claustrophobia ... none of them compare to the prospect of being fucked up the ass. Strangely enough, even though it is uppermost in everyone's mind when they think about prison, it is difficult to get anyone involved with prisons to talk about it. Wardens and guards will go so far as to deny that it happens, or give ludicrous explanations for it, generally pinning the blame squarely on the victim for making a mistake in judgment and hanging out with the "wrong" crowd.

Prisoners either dismiss it as unimportant or change the subject. Homosexuality is not something they like to admit to in the macho world of prison. And rape! They know that rape is so animalistic they also don't want to acknowledge it happens. It may have already happened to them. They may have done it. Certainly they've witnessed it and not done anything to stop it, and may feel guilty about that. Except to the most vile, rape is not something to be proud of. It's the last thing anybody connected with the prison system wants to discuss.

And it is never discussed during your "orientation."

So let's go to that first.

To the simple question "Am I going to get butt-fucked?" the simple answer is "yes." Sorry, the odds are not with you, Mr. Fish.

Conservative estimates indicate at least 290,000 males get sexually assaulted every year in prisons and jails. For a comparison, the Bureau of Justice estimates 135,000 women get raped each year in the whole country.

Both of these huge numbers are considered low. But they really don't compare with each other anyway. No woman who is raped in free society then has to become her rapist's permanent fuck or else be continuously abused by other rapists.

But the issue is (thankfully) not so simple as a yes-or-no answer. To the question of "How can I avoid getting butt-fucked" there are more complex answers.

The instances of knock-down, drag-'em-out rapes in prison are fewer and rarer than one might imagine given the media attention on the subject and the general perception of prison life. Your chances of being raped in jail are probably higher. Even higher than that are your chances of being raped at the Reception Center.

Still, you can make it through jail and "orientation" without too much trauma and then still have to face the same challenges in the big house.

The Nightmare

Remember the rec room converted into a dorm we discussed earlier? Once a prison becomes this overcrowded the chances of violence of every kind skyrocket. A room like this quickly becomes host to what is known as "the covered wagon." Prisoners arrange the three-high bunk-beds in a rough square and drape them with blankets to block off the view of the guards. It is in the middle of this that a gang rape can continue for an astonishing amount of time.

In 1973 a student protester didn't pay the $10 bail after being arrested at a Quaker pray-in at the White House where he was protesting the bombing of Cambodia. In the Washington, D.C. lock-up he was almost immediately attacked by fellow prisoners, sodomized and forced to suck dick while being nearly beaten to death for three solid days.

He was raped all day and all night. No guard came to his rescue. At one point he was so exhausted from the ordeal, his captors thought it wise to allow him some "rest" so he could continue being humiliated without dying. Another prisoner, in a twisted way, thought to try to make amends by offering the victim a carton of cigarettes.

This kind of violence happens most often in cellblocks which contain the most violent and bestial of prisoners who've been segregated away from the population. It's difficult enough to control these types as a group, using clubs and water hoses — trying to fine-tune their behavior is impossible.

Guys beaten and dragged into the covered wagon are set upon by dozens of men. They have all their teeth knocked out, they are forced to perform fellatio for hours and hours while being savagely fucked up the ass until their assholes literally gush blood. Even if the guards were able to detect what's going on (and they most certainly can), they would not do anything.

In fact, guards are almost always accomplices to this kind of mayhem and degradation for reasons we don't have room to get into here. Suffice it to say that guards are seriously-disturbed individuals. Whether they were born that way or became sadists as a result of their jobs might be debatable, but the fact of the matter is the guard is aware of each act of violence in a prison. He usually knows who did it.

It is little wonder that guards are routinely called "pigs" by prisoners and from now on in this book the words "guard" and "pig" will be used interchangeably. Don't worry about offending a guard by using this term. Chances are, he is so demented it wouldn't bother him anyway. Remember, this is a guy who goes to prison every day, by choice.

Back to rape...

Who's A Target?

Men who are already gay but don't want to choose a new boyfriend just yet are perhaps the most vulnerable to rape, and they will be beaten and raped as often as necessary until they seek protection — usually from the chief assailant himself. Thus, the only way for the man to stop being raped is to submit to the rapist. At that point he has become a "punk," and his life will be worse than wretched for the rest of his term in prison.

Once you've become somebody's fuck-boy, you stay a fuck-boy, and your new "man" will use you any way he wants. Soon he will send you out to perform sexual acts with other prisoners in exchange for a pack of cigarettes or some other bit of "currency" you'll then hand over to him. In exchange for his humiliation, the punk gets nothing. All the rest of the prisoners loathe the punk; the punk's master hates him, too. But at least he has some assurance that he will not be raped and beaten to death.

This is the reality of prison. The concepts of manhood and masculinity in prison bear only crude resemblance to those of the outside world. In prison, you are already a slave of the state, and punks simply become slaves to the slaves. Punks can (and are) bought and sold, or traded among prisoners.

Domination is the name of the game in prison, and the implications of allowing another man to "dominate" you in a sexual way are serious. The one who is "passive" (in prison lingo, the "catcher" as opposed to the "pitcher") is looked down on as less than a man, and consequently relegated to the bottom of the heap in prison status, only a half a notch above a snitch.

A punk has no rights, and once identified as such will be treated like shit for the rest of his bit.

The fact that the guy fucking the punk in the ass is also performing a homosexual act makes practically no difference in the prison scene.

He is "pitching" not "catching" and in most prisons, having a boy or two is a status symbol. If you're not gay and/or don't desire to become anyone's fuck-boy, you should be conscious of a few facts.

Kindness is taken as weakness in prison and weakness is seen as an indication that you can be "turned out." Prisoners sometimes view this rather revolting evolution in quasi-mystical terms. The sight of a man being abused beyond his ability to withstand it, of seeing a man's spirit being broken, is seen as a natural, even normal, phenomenon. Sure, they might recognize the violence of it, but they are no more offended by it than the outside world is "offended" by the violence of birth. Some prisoners have reassured themselves that what they are seeing is not an abomination, but a natural transformation some men must go through.

Once this transformation takes place, there is no turning back. Even a man who fought with all his might and suffered serious injury during a rape, is still suspect because he's been fucked in the ass. He has lost at least some, if not all of his manhood, he's slid to the bottom of the heap and will stay there. The possibility of coming back is almost nonexistent — although it is possible.

It would require a concerted and sustained fight with the whole fuckin' population, and the guards, to overcome. Physically overcoming it is the only way. This means a man may have to fight day after day for months or years, and probably will have to kill someone or be killed himself. Or get fucked in the ass.

As awful as life will be for the punk, some guys choose to accept it as a way of surviving — literally surviving, continuing to live — until their sentence is finished. They may think, "OK, I gotta suck dick and get fucked in the ass and get shit on by everybody in this prison, but I'm not telling anyone on the outside. And once I get out in two or three years, I'll put it behind me." And this is indeed a way that many men have coped with prison. To them, the humiliation and hell of being punked-out is not as bad as getting a lifetime sentence for killing someone or even being killed. It is an awful choice. But it's the only choice some guys get. And the choice is final.

Many just kill themselves. Those who live and are released re-enter society every bit as fucked up as you might expect.

OK, now that we've stressed the seriousness of the situation, let's get back to ways to avoid it.

Most guys who are "turned out" in prison are not turned out by a gang-rape. Most are essentially "seduced" into it by a "wolf" (a sexual predator). The wolf runs his prey in "a trick bag" of one sort or another.

One common one is that the "wolf," upon seeing a new guy frightened, without the little necessities of prison life, fresh out of "orientation," will stride up to the guy and be a friendly fellow. He'll pull up and ask the usual questions (What's your name? How much time you got? and, Hey, do you get high?) etc.

Yeah, sure you get high. Well, let's blow a couple joints then! Back in his cell he treats you to some dope and maybe you need some extra soap, squares (cigarettes), or coffee, too. Here, man, I'll give you some. Don't worry, you can lay them back on me when yours hits.

Of course, when you *do* score those things the wolf says that's not enough, that you "owe" him twice whatever he gave you, and he wants it NOW! or else it will double again. You may get a visit from one of his partners who'll come by your "drum" (cell) saying, "So and so wants his shit, so bring it out at chow."

Maybe he'll send someone to pick up his stuff for him and, of course, he never gets it. But you are the one in the wrong here because after all he gave the stuff directly to you, not through somebody else, so you shouldn't have sent it to him by nobody else! Where's my stuff?

All variations on this game have one thing in common: what looks like an easy way out of a bad situation — whether that's a debt you can't pay or a physical attack. The solution is to come simply on up to my cell at rec. and work something out.

"Like what?" "Well, like, you know — break me off a shot of ass."

"Hey, man, I ain't like that."

"Well then get my stuff then.

"Or, look, since you're not like that, you just jack me off. I won't tell anyone and then everything will be even — I'll even get you high."

Once you show you are scared and willing to negotiate along these lines, you'll soon end up "turned-out." If you jack him off, he can now use the threat of exposing your homo-act to get you to do more and more until you end up with a dick in your ass! This game may be played very discreetly, lasting over a period of months (time is hardly of the essence in prison), or it may be even more obvious and outright. The prison wolves have good instincts and can play every type.

So another basic rule is DO NOT borrow or accept anything from strangers when you get to prison. Don't refuse in a scared way, nor try to act "tuff." Just let it be known, if anyone asks, that you're "set" and pass on their offer. When they say, look man, I ain't runnin' no game, you say, you prefer to do for yourself, and that's how you do yours. Don't try to be "friends" with everyone or try to stay off in your cell like some snivelling coward ... just be yourself. If anyone tries to "punk" you (dictate to you or raise their voice to you), don't be cowed or intimidated... stand up for yours.

Often, when other cons see a new guy who will stand up and is still being abused, they will let the tyrants know to back off a little. If you must, don't hesitate to fight, or even more so, to kill. If you have to live in prison for any length of time you may as well do it on your terms and not as somebody's fuck-boy/slave. If it comes to a confrontation, stand your ground and fight to win. Your first impression will be a lasting one you must live with. Often, if it can be established that you're no punk, snitch, or push-over, you will not be butt-fucked. Be firm but not disrespectful to anyone and, again, don't be intimidated or act too "hard" ...prison is full of real killers, so such an act will be transparent.

Be observant of your surroundings, don't meddle in others' business, but be aware of who is who and be careful of who you associate with.

It's important that you stay on your toes the whole damn time you're locked up. You'd think that things would get better as the end of your bit approaches, but you're still in danger up until the time you walk out the gate.

One of the times when you're the most vulnerable is just prior to your release date. That's when the predators who have been reluctant to test you are apt to move in. They know that you don't want to get involved in any beefs that will attract the guards' attention. They'll assume that you'll be less likely to fight back and chance getting into trouble, which could mean getting written up and possibly extending your sentence. And they'll be right!

So watch your ass.

What If I Get Butt-Fucked Anyway?

In the event you do get raped and end up being sexually abused, or end up caught in some wolf's trick bag, there is P.C. (Protective Custody).

All you have to do is tell a guard you're having problems and you want to be placed on protective custody (sometimes called "check-in"). But this is definitely NOT recommended, as you will then be branded a punk and a coward. If you do go to P.C., don't compound your problems by snitching. If you were raped, say you don't know who did it, you didn't see their faces. Bringing the pigs into what is a personal dispute is a violation of the 11th commandment ("Thou shalt not snitch"). To inform on anyone — even the guy who fucked you in the ass — is to invite even worse treatment. If you're abused/raped, you can get some help if you can get access to a program to help you deal with it. See the Appendix for information on this subject and on rape prevention in prison.

Bear in mind that the prisoncrats are not at all sympathetic to your problem should you get fucked up the ass. They fear bad publicity and possible lawsuits, and about all they will do is put you in P.C. and try to get you to tell who did it. Besides, they may have been behind the thing in the first place. It's not uncommon for guards to deliberately lock a guy in a room with rapist/killers as a way of exerting control. The number of well-documented cases like this (sometimes called "cockfights") is staggering. The number of cases that you never hear of is even more so.

Just as in the streets, the pig is not your friend. Nobody at the prison cares about you in any way. Your captors do not consider anything they do to you to be wrong or excessive. Any exceptions to this rule are so rare as to be practically nonexistent. The guards are all half sadists ... yet they are perhaps the nicest of the prison staff! As you go up the ladder, they just get crueler.

Rape And Race

Rape, especially gang rape, is almost exclusively a black on white occurrence. More than 90% of prison rapists are black and the instance of a white raping a black is the rarest of all. If this rankles your ideals about racial harmony and the essential equality of the races, etc. — tough shit. Most rape victims are young and white. A 1989 statistic quoted in the *Washington Post* claimed one fifth of all prison murders are white men killing black "wolves." In Florida, the black on white rape problem has become so severe that white inmates have begun to sue the state for their failure to prevent it. Blacks do sometimes rape other blacks, however; if you're black, you're not in the clear.

Race relations in prison are worse than abysmal. There are books, college courses, whole careers devoted to the subject of race in prison. In some prisons, race is everything. If you are unlucky enough to be a white entering a large prison where young, aggressive blacks are in control and race war is continuous, you will be set upon very quickly by black guys who will try to get off in your ass. Being white in a prison like that is synonymous with being a punk.

In some cases this may happen within hours of your arrival.

Prisons rely on fomenting intense and violent hatred between the races in order to more easily rule the prisoners. Maybe they get some kind of sick jollies out of it. As far as race and rape go — there are explicit racial overtones that you cannot afford to ignore if you are imprisoned. Blacks commonly rape whites. That is that.

Another misconception about prison rape is that everybody gets raped. In fact, many feminist-idiots seem delighted with the poetic justice of a rapist being sent to prison and "getting some of his own medicine." Unfortunately this isn't the case. As on the outside, rape is a crime of violence — not sex. It's all about domination. So rapists on the outside tend to be wolf/rapists on the inside. There is some evidence that rapists are more subject to attack if they are perceived as somehow especially deviant, but since rapists are often naturally aggressive and violent, they soon adapt to their new role as prison wolf.

Furthermore, there is plenty of evidence that men who are raped while in prison become extremely violent once they are released into "civilized" society, and often rape women in a sick effort to regain their "lost" manhood.

A Way Out

Rape and other forms of violence happen in any prison in inverse proportion to the amount of time and effort the prison's administrators put into stopping it. If a prison warden decided that there would be no more rape in his prison, rape would essentially come to a halt. Even if just the guards decided to stop rape, they could end it at almost any time.

This is not to say the prisoncrats could stop homosexuality. That would be impossible because consenting participants would keep it hidden. In fact, a lot of prison homosexuals engage in fellatio more often than anal intercourse precisely because the latter is easier to detect. Guards would notice if two guys were fucking and might break it up if they thought they were enjoying themselves.

It goes without saying that the sort of hours-long assaults that frequently end in the beating or strangling death of the victim are well-known to the guards and other prison authorities even as they are happening. Often enough it is the prison "authorities" themselves who engineer just such an incident in order to consolidate power and intimidate the population. In the end the only person who can protect you is you.

You and perhaps some friends.

One type of person who does not get raped or otherwise fucked with is somebody with friends. Your reputation precedes you even on your way to prison. It is possible that the sort of crime you committed will help determine what sort of reception you'll get from your new neighbors. If you are a famous personality already popular with prisoners, you've got a big advantage since there will be guys in prison who will already stick up for you. If you're lucky enough to have this situation, make the most of it and be friends back. Don't get smug. Some popular film star might have some built-in protection right up until he gets smug. Then people might want to kick his ass just to show he's no better.

If you're a famous gangster, your chances of avoiding violence in prison are good. Of course to become a famous gangster you're going to have to be pretty violent well before you get there.

Rich people, too, might be able to buy their safety, but not by caving in to extortion. If you're known to have money, let it be understood that you don't pay for protection, but that you do use your financial power to punish your enemies and reward your friends. In the prison world, where two packs of cigarettes can be enough to hire a hit-man, a rich guy has potential power.

On the other hand, if you're a child molester, you've got serious problems in prison. This is one of the few generally-believed things about prison that happens to be true. People who commit heinous, cowardly crimes are targets. On the other hand, if you are considered to have been a courageous outlaw, so much the better.

One mistake made by fish is to assume that because they got through their first week in prison they're at least somewhat safe from being turned out. This person, of course, is ripe for a trick-bag or a seduction. He will make a grave error if he gets too confident. Many cons consider new prisoners to be fish for years after their arrival, and it's true — it takes years to get used to prison, to know your way around. If you show up in prison and manage to avoid a serious confrontation for a couple of months, know that the cons want it that way. Maybe you're not good-looking enough to jump on right away.

Or maybe they like you. Although you must keep your guard way up your entire time in prison, it is possible to make friends, just not for a good while after you get there. Remember you're on another planet here and even the all-important racial similarities (or even coming from the same neighborhood) cannot guarantee you allies. That comes only by being genuinely likable.

If you are the type who is afraid of violence, who would in a given situation, just for right now, prefer to blow a guy than get punched out, you're going to be a prison punk. If you are weak, you'll be fucked. It is unavoidable. Being a jerk will make you a target, too. Prisoners lead very high-stress lives and can become very irritated by the slightest thing, and violence is a cathartic way to blow off some steam in an acceptable (in prison) way. At the same time, prisoners are bored out of their skulls, so if you are of more value to other prisoners for what you already are (entertaining, interesting, informative, a good guy, whatever), there will be no reason to fuck you or otherwise dominate you.

I'll leave it at that. Even if you are "a little guy" you have the chance to make friends with other prisoners, so do it. It's a fine line between simple confidence and false bravado, but it's a line you must walk now. Be somebody other prisoners might like, but without threatening them. Too much confidence (acting "tuff") and you'll get your ass kicked just to see how easy or hard it is to do. "Little guys" who strike a sympathetic chord in other prisoners by showing themselves to be truly brave and maybe a little smart, won't get punked out, simply because that's not the best use of such a guy. You're never immune to attack, though, and if you ever start feeling that way, get your shit together quickly before somebody sees you swaggering.

Weapons

Because prison is a violent place, it is prudent to have a weapon — most prisoners do. And with a little creativity, a weapon isn't too hard to come by. Literally anything that is sturdy and can be sharpened down to a point, or used as a lead pipe, will work for a weapon. When you first get to prison, keep in mind that the guards aren't stupid. They know the first thing a new guy will do is get a shank ("hawk"), so expect them to shake down your cage within the first few weeks you get in a cell house. If you get a blank piece of steel or a steel rod, use your cell floor to sharpen it. Do this discreetly, otherwise you will undoubtedly be informed on!

You also may have the opportunity to buy a knife.

Be creative in hiding it, and realize your captors can be creative in searching. Getting caught with a weapon usually means you'll end up in the hole (disciplinary segregation), so it's also wise not to go around telling people you are armed. It's not even wise to go around armed until you know where the various check-points are inside the prison — places where you're likely to be patted down or made to walk through a metal detector, etc.

If you have a job, you may well have to go through such check points to and from work. In this case it's best to either have tools you can use as weapons at your workplace, or hide a weapon nearby. Remember, work locations are occasionally searched too, so hide it well. And, as before, don't tell anyone about it or it's likely to be stolen.

Most prisons have a few guns in them too, though you might not ever learn this unless you know someone who has one. Most common are "zip" guns made from metal tubes that fire a .22 caliber bullet. The firing mechanism can be made with a rubber band.

Gasoline or other flammable liquids are another common and effective weapon, and "torchings" are regular occurrences in prison. In a torching, a prisoner is usually trapped somehow (in his cell for instance) doused with a few gallons of gasoline and then ignited. That's that. When they come to get your corpse out, it will be charcoaled!

Knives can even be fashioned from plastic spoons — melted down and shaped correctly, these can be hard as stone. Another typical one is a razor blade melted into the end of a toothbrush, which then becomes a straight-razor and capable of inflicting serious harm.

For protection, prisoners make "bullet-proof vests." These aren't really bullet-proof but do provide some protection against stabbing. Vests like these are made from magazines wrapped inside a sheet, then wrapped and tied around the midsection.

When attacking someone, always wear a mask and gloves (masks can be as simple as pulling down a sweat-suit hood and flipping up a bandanna) and, as always, don't ever tell anyone. Destroy the weapon and as much of your disguise as possible. In fact, getting rid of any clothes with blood on them is essential. Most fights happen when lines of men are being moved around, such as to and from work, the yard, chow, etc. Fights like this usually don't last more than a couple of minutes before they are broken up by a guard. However, two minutes of fighting for your life will seem long enough! And if the fight happens in a more secluded area it can go on indefinitely. To avoid long-lasting fights, avoid isolation. Fights usually attract spectators and it's the massing of people that brings the guards.

Sex In Prison

Sex is rampant in prison, populated as they are by young men who might have a bit more testosterone than others in their age group.

AIDS is also rampant in prison, so indulge at your own risk. Most openly gay (that is, "effeminate") prisoners have a "man," but they are also well-known for their promiscuity (they're "dick-monsters") and often sneak around and get more dick elsewhere. Messing around with one of these guys not only exposes you to the highest possible risk for AIDS, but the news will eventually travel back to her boyfriend and then the consequences will be a bit more abrupt. Homosexual relationships in prison are often very emotional as well as physical, and the game of stealing each others' "boys" is an on-going drama in every joint.

Because of the intense ego/emotional factors surrounding these relationships, and the violent nature of prison, a lot of blood is shed over sissies. Most prisoners will tell you they think they've seen more violence related to homosexual mind-games than anything else. Do not underestimate anyone due to his sexual preferences. Don't think that the most effeminate of queens will hesitate to kill or defend herself. "Punks" and "sissies" do a lot of the killing in every sort of prison.

There is the microscopic possibility that you will be able to participate in some sort of conjugal-visit program, but that is so remote it's almost not worth mentioning. Of course, such programs would bring a rapid end to much of the sexual violence in prisons, but you're a prisoner and your place is to suffer.

Depending on your visiting situation, you may be able to make out with a girlfriend who comes to visit you, even feel her pussy or get a third-rate hand job, but probably not. In any event, you won't have any privacy at all. Other prisoners will oblige you by pretending not to see you, and guards might give you a little slack even if you do more than just kiss a few times, but you're still in full view of a lot of people.

Some prisons have female pigs, female clerical and medical staff, but these are off-limits. Look, but don't touch. And you *will* look, because they enjoy showing off for the guys. It's just more torment to add to your misery, pal!

Otherwise, it's going to be smut books and your imagination while you beat off for your whole stay in prison.

Gangs

Gangs and various other criminal organizations are rife in prison, just as you might expect in a place full of men convicted of crimes. In prison, though, it's taken even more seriously than on the streets. Mexican Mafia, Aryan Brotherhood, Black Guerrilla Family, Black Gangster Disciples, Vice Lords, Latin Kings, lots of different biker gangs and more are to be found in prison. Most of them are racially cliqued-up and very reactionary, with activities centered primarily around the drug trade. An old saying in prison is "whoever controls the drugs, controls the joint." Because getting high and staying that way is one excellent way to cope with prison, drugs are more than recreation, and any and every drug is in demand.

Gangs draw young, scared, new prisoners into their ranks, testing them by sending them to do something dangerous or perform some task for the gang. Some prison gangs have more organized structures than others and are able to function a lot like a real syndicate and thrive within the walls. Of course, this varies a lot from state to state and prison to prison. If you're not already in a gang, your best bet is not to join one once you come to prison. Once you're "in" you're not going to be able to just "get out." You could quickly find yourself a target of other prisoners from other gangs as well as your own, or even the prison administration. Prisoncrats regularly keep pressure on gangs by picking out one of the members and punishing him if someone from that particular group kills someone or commits another crime. Being in a gang opens you up to all kinds of folly, from combat and being physically attacked to facing new criminal charges for drug trafficking, murder and the like.

Jobs

Most prisons are terribly overcrowded. That means not everyone who wants a prison "job" assignment will be able to get one — and although work is hell, there are some advantages to it in prison. (Which shows you how twisted a world prison is!)

Jobs get you out of your cell during the day, which can go a long way toward shaping your otherwise empty day and keeping you from going literally stir-crazy. Jobs also provide you with (a very meager) income. State pay for inmates can be as little as a few cents per hour and varies from state to state and within the federal system. But jobs also give you a chance to "hustle" by pilfering stuff to sell in the cellhouse. Kitchen jobs, for instance, might give you the chance to bring back a nice steak, a glob of peanut butter or some other food that will be cherished by the other prisoners. You'll also get to eat better yourself (a serious problem in prison!).

Of course, you can also go to school (if your prison offers it) and even attend college or learn a trade. The classes are free except for a nominal filing fee, say ten or twelve bucks. Not only will you learn something by doing this, and keep from going insane in your cell, it looks good on your record and keeps you out of trouble. It's important to stay out of trouble since so many states have abolished parole and instituted what is known as "good time" in its place.

In systems with "good time," a prisoner is automatically given a certain amount of time off his sentence for every day he serves on good conduct. Often that's a day for a day. In some states it's even more! Keeping out of trouble in prison can cut your sentence appreciably. In some states, like Illinois, you can get two days taken off your sentence for each day you're "good." This means a twelve-year sentence can be cut to just four years, a four-year sentence to a little more than a year, and so on. Other systems, like the federal system, have also abolished parole but are not nearly so generous with "good time." The federal system, when it doesn't impose a minimum (as it increasingly does with each new "crime package") almost measures its time in minutes. A ten year sentence won't have more than a few months cut from it no matter how good you are.

So jobs or school can pay off in getting you the hell out of there faster, too. Fringe benefits show up, as well. If you're learning vocational electronics, you can fix radios for guys, get parts for their TV's, etc. In wood shops you can make shelves, cabinets, and furniture for men to put in their cells. Vocational auto shops can get you access to car speakers or anything else you find there. Guards' cars are particularly good pickings since they often hide dope behind the seats, and ripping off a guard's car just makes a guy feel better! Also, don't forget you've got access to gasoline now! Print shops have colored paper and inks for guys who make cards or make tattoos.

There are always license plate shops, which offer almost nothing to steal, but generally pay better.

Before you start cleaning out the place once you get on the job, check things out first. Of course you don't want to run the risk of getting caught, but you don't want to step on another prisoner's toes, either. See who is who at work. See who is who in any job.

Some jobs, like "pass runners" who have the run of the prison, or the guys working in the commissary (who get to pilfer along with their extra dividends paid to minimize pilfering!), or sweeping up the visiting room are key jobs. As such, they are coveted and competed for, so a lot of people are trying to get them.

Jobs like plumber, electrician, construction worker and so on are handy-man-type jobs that can put you in all sorts of places around the camp, giving you opportunities to scout out escape possibilities. Jobs like this might also let you facilitate cell transfers (for money) — to put a "man" and his "boy" in nearby cells for instance — by breaking a toilet or claiming a toilet is broken. Access to tools means you can do jobs in cells such as drilling holes in walls for shelves, or larger "fuck holes" for sex purposes.

Like everything else in prison, jobs are for sale and a choice job might be had for a carton or two of cigarettes, a bit of dope, anything.

Hustling

One of the primary occupations of prisoners is hustling to get by. Once in prison, aside from family support (which can be pretty shitty and tends to wane) and your "state pay" of $15 or $20 a month, most prisoners don't have any source of legitimate income. Of course, in some federal prisons there are millionaires doing time, but that's a rarity. So since a man still has a desire to get high, eat non-revolting food, etc., he is going to have to find some money. In some prisons, televisions and/or radios are allowed, but have to be purchased from the commissary and can cost a lot of money. Hustles are the only answer. Hustles can be broken down into two types: those that stay in prison and those that involve the outside world.

In-joint hustles center around the needs of your fellow prisoners, and we've touched on some of these needs already, but by far the biggest need of prisoners is to get intoxicated. Anything that will get you fucked up is valuable in prison and holds the potential for profit if you sell it.

Drugs

The biggest drug-hustle in prison is marijuana. It is usually smuggled in by a guard in relatively large amounts (¼ or ½ pound), then quickly broken down into very tiny pin-joints. A few grams, called a "piece," are bought for around $50, then fashioned into pin-joints, which come 5 to a "pack" or are sold individually. This sort of deal usually works out about as profitably as it does on the street — in relative terms. The seller will make enough to get high himself and maybe buy some chips at the commissary.

Of course, the weed trade can be very lucrative if you're higher up on the ladder and have front money, an outside connection and a pig who will bring it in for you. You've also got to be strong enough to set up shop. That means you've got to be mean. Welchers are everywhere, and dealers are almost besieged by people hanging around trying to talk them out of their dope. If you let a single guy get away with ripping you off, you're not only finished in the weed biz but your prison status drops to coward, and you'll be dealt with accordingly.

You can also become a prison brewmeister and make an alcoholic drink of varying quality and taste. Such hooch is normally judged only by its alcohol content anyway.

Prison hooch can be made in your cell toilet (as long as you don't mind using other peoples' toilets or finding some other solution), or, more often, in plastic trash bags. The recipe is simple: make a strong bag by double- or triple-bagging some plastic trash bags and knotting the bottoms. Into this, pour warm water, some fruit or fruit juice, raisins or tomatoes, yeast, and as much sugar as you can get ahold of (or powdered drink-mix). Now tie off the top of the bag, letting a tube of some kind protrude so the thing won't explode while it gives off carbon dioxide. Hide the bag somewhere and wait at least three days. A week is enough.

One of the problems you have right away with making wine in prison is the difficulty of getting yeast. It's a strictly forbidden item and you might not be able to get any. In this case, you can improvise the yeast by using slices of bread, preferably moldy (but not dry) and preferably inside a sock for easier straining.

If you choose to brew your wine in your cell, you'll need to hide it behind your bunk and do what you can to hide the smell. Burning cinnamon as incense is one way. Spraying deodorant around is another. Normal wine takes at least a month if not six weeks to make at all properly — but in hell, this is all you get.

Such alcohol is very popular and you can quickly sell this by the pint for smokes, food, reefer, and even green money!

Another intoxicant that's popular is an inhalant — sometimes called "tally water" — which is sold by the cough syrup bottle and "huffed." There are any number of solvents that will fuck you up if you breathe the fumes deeply, and some prison jobs will bring you into contact with them. Gasoline, too, can be huffed. So can shoe polish, paint thinner, various glues... any volatile petrochemical or solvent. Carbon tetrachloride is one of the stronger ones. Like modeling glue, it can produce truly mind-bending experiences that can render you flat-out stupid for hours. A few strong whiffs of the solvent and you can stare away at a wall for hours and hours! Well, it's better than being in prison!

Other prison-improvised drugs (which you can also prepare and sell) are huge overdoses of pseudoephedrine (Sudafed) — say 50 or 60 tablets — or Dramamine (say, a dozen hits). Dramamine overdoses can even be hallucinogenic, while Sudafed ODs are a kind of a speed-like head seizure. To strengthen the Sudafed high, it's wise to heat the pills (perhaps even boil them for a few minutes) on the off-chance that the heat will convert some of the drug to stronger compounds. Some guys have gone so far as to inject Sudafed. Mixing it with caffeine has a synergistic effect.

Of course, "hard drugs" are available in prison, too. Normally these get smuggled in by visitors who pass them to inmates inside balloons no bigger than an almond M&M. The prisoner waits till near the end of the visit, takes the balloon and swallows it, then goes through the whole strip-search routine (including the asshole peek). Back in his cell he can barf it out or, if he can't do that, grab it on its way out the other end. Given prison diets of starch and more starch, this can take up to a week, and you will have to dig through your shit until you find it.

Drug paraphernalia is also in big demand in prison. A syringe is worth quite a lot, for instance. Decent rolling papers and plastic bags are other examples.

Tattooing is another good gig in prison if you can draw. Tattoo guns are made using slot car motors brought in via pig/mule (courier) or otherwise, and attached to AC lamp cords or batteries for power.

Hint: it's possible to make a water heater out of a lamp cord and two razor blades. Attach one blade to each wire, then glue the blades together with a thin shim of wood or cardboard between them. Plug it in and it will sizzle. Drop it in water and it'll boil. You also might short out the whole wall. Nowadays a lot of prisons allow "stingers," small water-heating elements.

Another improvised cooking technique is to burn rolls of toilet paper and hold whatever you want to cook over the fire with a coat-hanger wire. You may have to fashion a flue to draw the smoke out a window to avoid being busted by the pigs or attracting other unwanted attention.

Inks for tattoos can be gotten through the prison's own arts & crafts program or made by burning plastic into a soot and mixing it with water. Prison tattoos, sometimes called "scratch," can be really bad, so a man with a tattoo gun and a good eye for reproduction, or an artistic flair, can do well. Tattooing is, of course, forbidden, so it's got to be done on the sly, a little bit at a time each day until finished. The guy getting the tattoo takes pains to cover the thing while it's in progress and until it heals up, so he won't get busted and thrown in the hole.

Artistic guys can also make some money by making gift cards or other items, like jewelry boxes made out of popsickle sticks, which can be sold for amazing amounts of money ($20-$30!), and which are often re-sold by prison-affiliated groups in the outside world. Gift cards sell for around a pack apiece. (You provide the envelopes, too!) Prisoners also like to have paintings done of their families or their old lady, and drawings or paintings like these can be a steady source of decent income. Here again it's important that you aren't "nice" and do free work for anyone. Once you do something for free, then everyone else will want it free, and could get very offended that they have to pay. That'll put you out of business and throw you into another confrontation.

If you really feel like a tough guy you could also try running a "store." But you've got to be both strong and diligent... and have enough capital to store up a lot of commissary items/smokes, etc. The store then "loans" an item at the usual prison rate of 100%. In this case, the customer has to pay back twice whatever he bought on the next commissary day, with commissary usually run weekly. The store serves mostly to tide guys over until commissary, and people just get an item here or an item there.

It's important not to let anyone get in over their head; if someone doesn't pay on time, the debt doubles again and you've got to enforce it. Running a store can be a headache and unprofitable if you don't have the respect of your fellow prisoners, and, of course, there will always be those one or two welchers who can't or won't pay. It will usually be over a very petty amount, say two or three packs, but by now you know you're in a tough position. You can't lose face, and yet there's no sense in killing or harming someone over it, so that guy just gets no more credit from the store. But, as a welcher, he's probably fucked over more than one guy and will eventually pay the penalty for it .

Most joints have regular "store-men" who run stores year-in and year-out, and there may be two or three stores in the same cellhouse.

Selling sandwiches is another good hustle. To do this, you buy a hot-plate (or make one), and arrange a connection in the kitchen for hamburger, cheese, lettuce, mayo, ketchup, mustard, etc. Burgers made-to-order sell for a pack apiece, and you can turn an excellent profit. Most places, you can buy a styrofoam cooler from the commissary, and ice is passed out regularly, so you can keep your supplies cold. Of course, you'll have to give the pig in your tier/section a sandwich now and then to keep him from hassling you about the hot plate and illicit food in your cooler. This is typical of guard/prisoner relationships. At times, in some prisons, guards have been known to sleep through their shifts, snoring quietly in the knowledge that if anything happens or a supervisor is on his way, his prisoner pals will wake him up in time. The love/hate relationship between prisoners and guards is sometimes confusing.

You can also run gambling pools on football games, host card and dice games in your cell, or any other form of gambling. But make sure you have the money to cover your debt or don't go near any betting. This is survival, and you must never depend on money that's owed to you being paid back in time for you to pay your own debts. If this constant advice to watch your step in the exchange of any type of good seems petty, that's because it is. Prison reduces men to their lowest form — it's as vicious as you would expect a bunch of caged, tormented, frightened and aggressive men to be. Hence, having bones broken over a snack-size pack of potato chips is to be expected.

This point about watching your step and watching your back cannot be stressed enough when it comes to surviving in prison. It's like that for everyone in prison. If prisoners ever felt they could be honest about such a feeling, they would readily admit there are few times when they can really relax. It's not going to be any different for you.

Hustling The Outside World

Every now and then you read in the newspaper about how some convict was caught orchestrating some type of scam from prison. Being imprisoned in no way stops many guys from continuing to perpetrate crimes — prisoners have even arranged for murders to take place. It all depends on getting someone on the outside to cooperate. And there are a few people in the outside world who are still vulnerable to a good con, no matter how deep and far away he's locked up.

Normally, hustles connected to the streets are centered around confidence games, credit card schemes, altering money orders (another type of work for the budding artist to try his hand at) or some other way of using your own imprisonment to your advantage. Book-of-the-Month Club-type offers are constantly getting ripped off by prisoners who simply sell the books or records they get and bust out laughing when the companies send them letters demanding payment.

These cons know all they have to do is alter their names by one letter on the next postage-paid offer they send in to rip off the same companies over and over. As a prisoner, you should never lack for reading material, thanks to these book clubs!

One of the oldest games in the joint is writing to homosexuals or lonely women. In fact, if you're a famous prisoner, you're likely to already have groupies — women who get off on being attached to a felon. These women willingly do whatever the con asks of them — he doesn't even have to bullshit them! Even if you're not famous, there are a lot of pathetic souls out there that are just waiting for the chance to get ripped off. Here's how you can help.

Although you can answer an advertisement in a lonely hearts/queer mag or paper, you'll have the best luck if you put in an advertisement yourself. You can even pose as a woman. If the correctional facility doesn't specify the gender of its prisoners, it's easy to be a woman. Simply pick a girl's name and — as a photo — send either a pic of a real girl, or of a woman's face cut out of a magazine, then xeroxed over and over. This is how prisoners send out their pictures a lot of times anyway, since they don't have access to cameras and film.

Horny guys believing they've latched onto a hot chick behind bars are just as happy to blunder into the trap as any fag or woman. So this is an equal-opportunity scam.

In any case, you can quickly become pen pals with many different people. Slowly, you bring them along until you get them to pay a bill for you or to send some money. Then you up it and keep upping it... but slowly. All the while your pen pal relationship escalates into "I love you, darling," and the pen pal starts to think his or her dreamboat has arrived. They dream of someday (Oh God, let it be soon!) hooking up with their ill-fated soul-mate. It really doesn't matter if he's got 50 years. Though it helps to claim you'll be getting out soon, the fact that you're never getting out can be easily forgotten by your prey. If you doubt this, just think back on some of the stupid things you have already done while in love!

And make sure to establish and nourish as many of these relationships as you can. Having 20 or more such pen pals is not too many!

All sorts of reasons can be contrived to get money, from supposed legal courses, to purchasing a T.V., to whatever (my gym shoes got stolen ... boo hoo!). Master the art of "sob script" and you're on your way to a fatter bank account. As the date nears for your supposed release, you can get even more money. Best of all is to tell the pen pal that you stand a much better chance of getting out early if he/she would only send $1,500 (or more!) to help pay off a lawyer or get something filed by a jailhouse lawyer. Be creative! Use your imprisonment to your advantage in these letters, and keep the bullshit coming. With a constant stable of a couple dozen pen pals you'll have a full schedule of letter-writing to do, but you'll wonder why the hell you didn't do this before when you were free.

Of course, money means power, and you might really be able to use that money to get out. Of all the people in the world who could use a few bucks, none need it more than a prisoner.

Another scheme is to alter postal money orders. Although post offices all over the country have little signs up warning of this scam, and lots of prison mail is stamped with alerts for forged money-orders, it still works. Here's how:

A good forger can take a money order for $1.00 and transform it into a money order for $691 (or whatever the limit allows). These are then sent to unsuspecting pen pals to cash and send either to you, the prisoner, or somewhere else. Of course, it doesn't matter if the pen pal gets caught (they often do). The con is already looking at hundreds of years, and his main concern is not catching more time, but staying high! In fact, a little trip to court to be convicted of more crime might be diverting. Millions of dollars a year get sent to prisoners this way.

Another outside scheme is played by having someone (pen pal maybe?) order you a pair of gym shoes to replace the ones stolen by that meanie. It's easier by mail anyway. The shoes, of course, arrive with the invoice, which bears the credit card number of the pen pal. Now the prisoner can use this number to call in (or write) orders for whatever they want — jewelry, clothes, ant farms, it doesn't matter. When the stuff arrives, the prisoner is going to be asked to "mail it home," as such items as ant farms are forbidden to prisoners. No problem! Mail the ant farm to your old lady and have her sell it or trade it for drugs, or just sit there and admire the ant farm her man so creatively provided for her.

Once again, the least of a prisoner's worries is getting caught. After all, what are they going to do? Throw him in jail? As it is, the victim will go ahead and pay the bill and nothing more is said of it. If you've got a particularly good pen pal, you might be able to feign sorrow for what you've done, get forgiven — then do it again!

The same trick that works for book clubs also works for magazine subscriptions. By mailing back those "bill me later" cards you'll start getting *Time* and *Newsweek* and *Ant Farms Today* for a good two or three months before they finally stop sending it. After that, you get the letters demanding payment, and then it stops. Don't worry, they can't and won't do anything to you except notify the credit agency. (Oh no, not that!) Meanwhile, just change one letter in your last name and do it again. Smith becomes Smitth becomes Smit then Smiith then Schmidt and on and on, and the publication's computers will keep treating it as a new subscription each time.

To ensure that this works, it's best to have someone on the outside mail them, as prisons often rubber stamp outgoing mail and these are often (but not always) thrown out by the magazines. Some prison mail rooms even have the audacity to not mail them out!

With the new ability to incorporate by phone for $50 (paid for by a pen pal's credit card?) a whole new world of fraud opens up to the prisoner.

Phone Calls

Because all phone calls made from prison have to be collect, you're going to have trouble. For instance, you can't call 1-800 numbers. The best way to get around this problem is to make an arrangement with a friend on the outside to have three-way calling installed and accept your phone calls. It is also possible for a friend to leave a message on his or her machine accepting all collect calls from you so that you can leave a message if necessary.

Phone-calling is a privilege and is one of the first to be taken away as a punishment.

Pets

Although it's being phased out, many prisons allow prisoners to keep pets, and those that don't have guys keeping them anyway. Most common are cats and fish. Where pets are being phased out, they've only stopped prisoners from ordering new ones. This means that you can buy the offspring of those animals grandfathered-in, and you could even become a pet breeder. Imagine finding a new calling in life as a guppy breeder in prison! Maybe someone will even make a movie about you someday — *The Fishman of Folsom*!

Even where they're not allowed, lots of prisons have cats in them. There's not much anyone can do about it. Prisons are full of tasty rats and mice, and what with those hundred-year-old walls inside the labyrinth, there are going to be cats. Illicit pets might be a cat or mice or rats or even cockroaches. It's a strange, even tender phenomenon, but even in the bowels of hell, man still likes company. Once again, as a prisoner, you're stripped of your humanity and are reminded every day you are loathed and scorned and less than human. Having a pet can be that one pinprick of hope in this world.

Hobbies

Aside from arts & crafts, there are several other activities you can take part in to while away your time and preserve some measure of your sanity. The musically-inclined can hook up with the prison band. Some places even allow you to have a musical instrument in your cell. Sports groups of all kinds exist, and body-building is beyond a fetish for some people behind bars.

By far the most popular "hobby" is watching TV, which is encouraged by your captors. As a drug, nothing can compete with TV. It's cheap, completely mind-numbing, and keeps the user immobile and dumb. Don't be surprised if you end up a TV-addict in prison. Prisons with televisions playing constantly in day-rooms are packed with guys watching installments of their favorite soaps. Crime shows, especially the "real-life" cop shows, are popular too, as each episode generates critique and discussion among the watchers as to how the perpetrator could have better done his crime, or noting law enforcement techniques. Sports too, are on a lot. Sometimes a single TV will be devoted to sports (since, at any given time of the day, there is at least one form of "ball" on). MTV is another popular channel, where the prison has cable.

People on the outside may rant and rave about "mollycoddling" prisoners by allowing access to TV, but prison administrators know it's as good as thorazine for keeping otherwise dangerous men relatively docile.

A far better way to occupy your time is by reading and learning. Almost every prison has a library, and regular access can be obtained by sending a "request slip" to the librarian for a pass. Prison libraries can also make use of inter-library loan programs to give you access to books they don't have. Most college presses and other book publishers will send a few free books to prison libraries if asked, and many outside organizations specialize in providing various books (often of religious or political nature) to prisoners. Political groups on the left, and some on the right, will send their newspapers for free. Sign up for all you can. While they may not share your political outlook, it's a good and free source of news otherwise unavailable.

It's possible for you, as a prisoner, to become one of the more well-informed members of society. Some prisons (like Louisiana State Prison in Angola) even publish their own newspapers, and there are even a few prisoners who publish zines. Zines, too, are often free to prisoners. See Appendix for addresses.

Even if your prison doesn't have a newsletter of sorts, writing is still another great pastime. You'll discover tons of little magazines that will help you to get even your poems into print. And there are more than a few publications that are genuinely interested in a prisoner's point-of-view — about anything. Even establishment newspapers have been known to publish prisoners' letters and articles. One famous case is Danny Martin, who, for a long time, wrote about prison life for the *San Francisco Chronicle*.

That was fine as long as he didn't write about too much that was controversial. When he reported on a prison riot from the inside (an intensely interesting point-of-view), he was suddenly forbidden to write for the *Chronicle* anymore, and, when he persisted, was "put on the bus" to be shuttled around California prisons in an attempt to shut him up through the sheer weight of bureaucracy. Prison moves are notorious as punishment. Not only is your hard-won "life" turned upside down and you've got to start all over again, your mail will be "lost" for weeks, if not months.

Another well-known prison writer was Jack Abbott, who essentially ran the lonely-hearts game on Norman Mailer, who got him published and then sprung from jail. Mailer personally vouched for Abbott and took him from a lifetime of savagery at the hands of society into the heart of the New York Elites. Abbott went from "the belly of the beast" to "radical chic." Apparently, life as Mailer's ape-on-a-rope, performing for the white-wine-and-weekends-in-Europe set, wasn't good enough for Abbott. He was soon back in prison, this time for life, when he stabbed a busboy to death for some perceived slight in a restaurant.

That little episode sums up a lot about this part of the book. It shows the potential benefits of writing letters (or writing anything at all) — after all, it got the guy out of prison! It made him rich and famous!

And the story also shows the intense ferocity of prison culture. That busboy Abbott killed probably had done something worthy of being stabbed to death had he been in prison. But he *wasn't* in prison, and neither was Abbott. On the outside, especially in New York, the busboy may not have been perceived as rude or even impolite. As seen by a prisoner, he was a dead man.

Once again, it illustrates the lesson of watching your step every minute of every day. Prison is full of Jack Abbotts, whether they want to be or not. If you spend much time there, you'll become a Jack Abbott, too.

Actually, given the confinement and time to reflect, a prison can be a place of self-awareness and spiritual growth — provided the prisoner can pull free of the madness and hustle of prison life. While religion is (or should be, anyway) a way of life for us all and not a "pastime or hobby," it is a positive way to occupy one's time and can have a balancing effect on one's life — pretty important given the extremes of the prison environment.

Many, many prisoners go looking immediately for God when they find themselves in prison. Bereft of everything in the world except his pain, even the most "atheistic" guy will look for God. Your chance to join a religion or to become religious is right there when you get to prison. The two most common religions in prison are Christianity and Islam. Both of these religions are misperceived by many inside and outside prison.

The Christianity found in prison is not at all like the lukewarm northern Presbyterian church where the pastor tries to slip a few Bible verses into his sermons about forgiving the guy who cuts you off in traffic. Prison Christianity is Bible-banging, charismatic religion. And it is officially sanctioned by the authorities. In keeping with that approval, Christian ministers are given plenty of access to the sinners locked up inside, and prisoners are encouraged to talk to them. Indeed, a minister may well be the only person who bothers to visit a guy locked up in a cage.

The Bible is the one book they always let you keep in prison, even in the hole. Right up to the fucking electric chair, they provide you with some kind of Christian authority figure to accompany you to your death.

Especially to the most wretched of the wretched — the child molesters, the punks — this Christianity offers some refuge. They will not beat you up, they probably will not butt-fuck you. They will forgive you when no one else will. In return, they ask only that you reaffirm your wretchedness and admit to them that you deserve what you get. If you can abase yourself enough to them, they will give you the psychic strength to withstand abasing yourself some more elsewhere.

There are, however, plenty of good Christians in prison — it's just that these guys aren't from the "approved" schools of thought and aren't immediately apparent. Eventually, most prisoners lose any affinity for the kind of religion they are offered by the authorities. After all, it doesn't explain how in the fuck this happened, and it's not going to get them out. So, unfortunately, a lot of prison Christianity remains the scene of child-molesters and other broken men who have given up hope.

Islam is commonly thought to be a "blacks only" religion and, indeed, the Nation of Islam *is* "blacks only." They see the white man as a kind of demon, and have their own theories about racial superiority that are every bit as bizarre as the Aryan Nation's. Like the white racists, they seek refuge in their skin color and tell each other how their misery is the fault of another race.

Except for using words like "Allah" for God and the name "Islam" for their religion, the Nation of Islam has nothing to do with Islam as it is practiced by the billion or so Muslims of the world.

Islam is a universal faith. Its foundation is the Koran. One of the reasons it is popular in prison is it offers men a way out. Muslims have an advantage if they follow their religion, which discourages homosexuality, forbids borrowing and lending (at any interest) and encourage other behaviors that can protect a prisoner from becoming a ruthless animal. Muslim communities in prison are very tightly knit and tend to take care of their own.

At the same time, don't join up with Muslims just for protection. Muslims will not long tolerate an impostor or one who constantly breaks the rules of the religion.

But religion, real religion, is alive and well in American prisons. Some joints have many kinds of religious activity — Zen Buddhism, Taoism, Native American religions, and Islamic "dhikr" all offer forms of meditation to those seeking a way to unwind, find inner strength, and maybe even some peace and quiet.

Literature about all these faiths is available, and to get it you only need to ask someone involved in these various religious communities and they'll be happy to accommodate. The Appendix also lists some places you might contact on these matters.

Church services are held on Sunday mornings in most prisons — choir, Bible-study and similar activities are held at different times — just ask the chaplain about them. Islamic services are on Friday afternoons, with other activities taking place at other times. To find out about Muslim affairs, see just about any Muslim prisoner in your cell house. Theoretically, you can also ask the chaplain, though he may take the opportunity to try to save your soul and try to talk you out of going to Muslim services.

Various other clubs and organizations also exist in prison without much hassle from the authorities. There are the Jaycees, the Lifers Club, Nam Vets Associations, and other organizations normally doing positive things for prisoners. Though prisons have a lot of savages in them, they also have a good number of sincere and well-meaning cons who are trying to improve conditions of prisons. There are also African-American, Latino, and American Indian cultural groups and study classes, which can be very positive experiences for you.

If there is one thing that can save you from becoming a savage it is nourishment of the spirit. We encourage you to look for God... not a man, God.

4
Jailhouse Justice

Isolation

What do they do to you if you're bad in prison? After all, there must be an answer to the rhetorical question, "What are they gonna do, throw me in jail?"

The answer is basically, yes, they'll throw you in jail. You go to prison within prison — isolation, lock-up, the hole.

This kind of isolation or segregation ranges in intensity from simply being confined to your cage all day, every day, in a different part of the prison, to being nearly buried alive in a sound-proof room with no light.

The former is designed to drive you a little stir-crazy but you can still communicate with other prisoners in the segregation unit by yelling down the range. You can even sometimes come into contact with other prisoners during the half-hour or hour they let you out of your cell to mill around the tier or take a shower. And you can read. You'll have to, since you'll lose your TV, radio, tape player, etc.

The latter is far worse. Man is a social animal and no matter how stoic you might think you are, loneliness and isolation can become intolerable if they get bad enough. People who are thrown into solitary confinement and never communicated with become very agitated very quickly. If you can believe it, most people would rather live in a world of dirt and mayhem than be shut up in a box all alone.

In fact, the most notorious prisons, the ones considered the most inhumane in the United States, are not at all the most "dangerous." Marion Federal Prison, which has served as a model for new prisons over the past ten years, is the prototype of this new kind of prison. It's not dirty, and your chances of being beaten or raped by fellow prisoners are nearly zero. It's also the only federal prison that provides — at no cost to the prisoner — a color TV in each cell.

But such maximum-security prisons are feared because of the utter sensory deprivation that can be brought down on the inmate within minutes. In fact, were it not for the color TV, a prisoner in this type of cell would be so cut off from the world as to drive him almost immediately insane.

These cells are located underground and no natural light reaches them, ever. The temperature is controlled by the guards (who can make it hot or cold as they see fit), and there is no talking between prisoners or guards. Every day, a trio of guards come, truss you up with handcuffs and leg irons tied together with a nylon leash and, "rib spreader" (club) pressed against your side, shuffle you to the shower or to a treadmill inside a steel mesh cage for exercise.

Of course, you're probably not going to Marion, so you might just get tossed naked into a concrete box with a hole in the middle of the floor. They'll give you a Bible, but you won't be able to read it because as soon as the solid-steel door slams shut, it's completely dark. From time to time food is pushed through a slot. Nobody talks to you. Go ahead and scream, go ahead and cry. If the temperature starts to rise and you feel the walls closing in around your throat, your cries will not be heard. No amount of pleading will open that door before the guards feel like opening it.

You might stay there forever, too, since you may have a sort of indeterminate sentence down there. You might get out in five minutes and you might not get out for the rest of your life. Soon, the difference between five minutes and forever is moot. It already seems like forever. It is eternity.

Suicide, if you can figure out how to do it, seems a reasonable option. It is very common for prisoners in isolation to suffer from vivid and horrifying hallucinations, extreme panic, and delusions of bizarre and continuous persecution as their minds turn on them.

So how do you get to this place?
By breaking the rules.

Rules

Every prison has a set of rules and policies that govern how you're supposed to behave while held captive. Usually you will have been issued a rule book of some sort back at the reception center, or at least during "orientation." It's important to study these rules very carefully, as they constitute the regime you will have to live under. Breaking the rules has serious consequences.

In addition to any of the rules in the book, there are verbal orders given by a guard that have the immediate force of a rule. You must obey the guards.

Of course, prisons vary. Some are very strict and enforce even the pettiest of rules with vigor. Others are more open, and no rules are enforced beyond those absolutely necessary to keep you in prison. More often than not, guards will tend to turn their heads at minor infractions, and some will only write you up ("give you a shot," "ticket you") if you "put them on front street"; that is, if you openly defy them, especially if another guard is around.

There are always those guards who are so gung-ho they're like bulldogs. Some of these guys get off on ordering prisoners around and it's best to stay away from them. In fact, it's good policy not to flout the rules in front of any guard, if you want to keep on doing what you desire, without getting caught or letting the rules impinge too much on your life. So don't act stupid in front of any guard and don't ever let your captors know what you're doing, or how.

Should you get busted for making wine, possession of a knife, getting into a fight, or any other infraction, you should expect to be given a write-up or "conduct report." If your offense is serious enough you might be immediately confined to your cell ("red-tagged") until you go before the prison disciplinary board for your hearing over the matter.

Even in prison, you are entitled to "due process" — even if it's only a kangaroo court. In fact, this "due process" may seem petty to someone on the outside, but it is extremely important to the prisoner. The deck might be stacked heavily against him, but these in-prison trials and investigations become every bit as serious (in outcome) as their counterparts in the free world. This is part of the very thin veneer of civilization that remains in prison.

The guard's write-up is given to the shift supervisor who approves it and turns it over to "screening." Then, usually within 5-7 days at most, you'll be sent a pass to go to have your offense explained by the screening officer. If you've been red-tagged, the screening officer comes to your cell.

At the screening you get a copy of the write up, and are read your rights, and asked if you have any witnesses who you want to be given passes to appear at your hearing. You'll also be told the date and time of your hearing and asked if you want a Lay Advocate to go with you. A Lay Advocate is usually another prisoner who knows the rules and can act as a sort of attorney for you at the hearing. This is the minimum due process as stipulated by the U.S. Supreme Court, so no matter where you're incarcerated, this is the least you can expect. It's also likely to be the most you can expect.

Depending on what state you're in, you'll appear before a hearing board or a hearing officer. At this hearing you have the right to call witnesses, to speak on your own behalf, to present evidence and to know what evidence is being used against you (usually you'll be informed of this at the screening). You are also to receive a written conclusion explaining what the screening officer and/or board has decided and why.

If you're found guilty (and the chances of that are good), you can appeal to the warden and then to the Department of Corrections' central office/Commissioner. If you keep getting found guilty, you can then file an appeal in both state and federal courts challenging the findings. This is especially true when "good time" is at stake or your "time class" is otherwise altered.

Theoretically, this means you could go to the Supreme Court over a beef about having food in your cell. In practice, this isn't going to happen because higher courts will not normally rehear evidence unless you show the guilty finding was not based on at least some showing of fact. The court will merely look to see whether or not any of your due-process rights were violated. Those rights include the hearing where you were found guilty, so don't pin your hopes on Sandra Day O'Connor delivering an impassioned finding on the food you had in your cell.

Once found guilty, you'll be sanctioned. That means punished. By reading the rule book you'll usually be able to tell what can or will be done to you for violating a given rule. Sanctions can vary from a verbal or written reprimand ("don't do that again!") to tougher actions such as restrictions on phone, recreation, commissary, or other privileges. You also face the possibility of having your "good time" taken away and/or being thrown in the hole.

These last two things are pretty serious. Taking away good time effectively allows a guard to add time to your sentence by writing you up for some rule infraction. The hole speaks for itself.

Because of this you might consider pleading guilty at your hearing in the hopes of a lesser sanction. Some Lay Advocates can horse-trade like public defenders to get the disciplinary board to cut a deal. Some prisons are so corrupt that you can also buy, literally buy, a not-guilty verdict or have "good time" restored, or cause your hearing to be delayed beyond the 5-7 day screening-period so as to result in an automatic dismissal.

Sounds like the same process that got you here in the first place, no?

If you're facing a hearing, the best advice is to work out some half-way reasonable excuse or lie to explain the matter or at least cast some doubt on the issue. You can say it was only a jug of orange juice they confiscated, but of course it's fermented now since it's been held as evidence for the past week.

Your Lay Advocate can help you make up a decent lie, one that won't seem too outlandish or piss off the authorities. Your defense should be along the lines of "I really wasn't wrong... no, the guard isn't lying — he just misunderstood what I was doing or saying." You should expect the pig's word to be taken, but this kind of spiel can help mitigate the sanction from the hearing board.

Bear in mind, though, when caught in a fight, going in and saying "he hit me first" or something similar is the same as snitching — which has its own sanctions.

In this case it's best to have your Lay Advocate get with the other guy's attorney and work out statements to help each other. Now you both say, "We were just horse-playing and rough-housing and the guard over-reacted." If your opponent won't co-operate for some reason, then at least keep silent and hope your Lay Advocate can find a technicality somewhere. Just don't snitch. Even if someone tells on you, that's not enough reason to snitch back. Snitching is snitching.

This brings us back to the central subject of survival in prison and the paramount importance of adhering to certain prison "ethics."

Beyond the "don't ever snitch" commandment are other concepts to keep in mind.

It is also best never to label anyone — anyone — a snitch unless you know for certain that it's true. The same goes for saying someone is gay or anything else that could be viewed as "unmanly" in prison. To call somebody a queer or a snitch when it's not true can get you killed.

By the same token, if anyone should label you something like that, and does it openly, you should respond in deed ... failure to aggressively correct such bullshit will result in the label sticking! Gossip is rife in prison — the "grapevine" is everywhere and in constant use. But it's best to listen only, and don't spread or pass on any of it. You can run yourself up in a trickbag quickly by talking or gossiping. Your mouth can get you in serious trouble.

Never say something about someone behind their backs that you wouldn't say in their presence. Never, ever, say out loud to anyone anything you don't want others to know you know or otherwise reveal even a hint of your secrets. The old saying that "there are no secrets in the penitentiary" is true.

Also, watch everything else you say. You've also got to keep your word in prison — you're going to live and die by it, so don't get into the habit of lying or "war-storying" about your exploits and capers. In fact, it's best to keep anything personal to yourself — completely! Don't give other prisoners the addresses or phone numbers of any of "your people" (your wife, parents, etc.). Tear off return addresses before throwing away envelopes. Pick your associates carefully and on your own. Always do your own thinking.

Don't "jeff" (joke, play) with the pigs. They are your captors and not your friends or laughing buddies. Don't disrespect anyone and don't tolerate anyone "dissin'" you. Don't get into the habit of making threats, either, and if you are ever threatened, take it seriously and do whatever you have to to preemptively protect yourself. Don't leave anything laying around or unlocked that you don't want stolen. New guys, especially, are preyed upon due to their lack of awareness of the prison value system.

That's why you should also refrain from allowing people to constantly beg off you. A new guy will at times give out more coffee and squares than he will use... no doubt not wanting to say no or seem petty, not realizing that other people are petty enough to keep coming back. They might even start getting mad if you try to stop giving them things.

Tell these guys, "I don't mind, but you need to spread your shots a little" — it's an easy way to let it be known that you don't appreciate the constant mooching.

Of course, it has to be said again, never borrow anything unless you know for certain you can pay for it on time. Don't depend on someone who owes you coming through — that's counting chickens before they're hatched. Be sure you have the means to cover any debt, and depend on only yourself for those means.

Just as there are a hundred and one "hustles" you can use to get by in prison, so are there plenty of prisoners making their livings by being "rustlers" and preying on each other — especially on new guys. Beware of petty schemers, beggars, and thieves.

And never, NEVER tell on anyone or go to the pigs with one of your problems or disputes involving other prisoners. You've got to solve your problems by yourself like a man. There is an old convict saying that goes "Drink plenty of water and walk slow... the water will keep your system flushed and you're going nowhere fast!" Take it to heart. Prison time goes by very slowly and yet every little move you make can have consequences.

Prisoners tend to run in cliques based on shared interests or coming from the same regions. But don't automatically trust someone or accept them as "okay" just because he's your "homeboy" or claims to know some of the people you do (watch out for "name-droppers"). And don't let anyone know your business. This can't be said enough times. The tiniest shred of information can be blown up or extrapolated and used against you. The name-dropper, for instance, may have never met the people he claims you know in common, but some guys are very clever at picking up information and piecing things together. Remember how important it was not to tell anyone the truth when you were first in custody? Same goes in prison, and it goes for the duration. To keep your business your business means never talking about it.

Piss Tests

Most prisons have piss-test programs to monitor drug use. If you're "dirty" you can take the test and get popped, or you can refuse to take the test and get popped. If you're sure you're "dirty," it's best to refuse the test. You will be written up and likely punished with the same sanction you would have gotten had you tested positive for drug use, but it won't be on your record that you're a drug user. That can have broad implications when it comes to parole considerations, etc.

The best way to refuse is to say you can't piss. Tell 'em you've got "shy kidneys" and you just can't do it. You'll be written up, but it gives you a chance to stay clean for the next few days until your hearing, when you can explain your dilemma. Ask to be found not guilty because it's not your fault, and offer to be retested right then. They won't do it, but you might get off anyway. If you do get off this way and they don't test you that day, be prepared for them to show up in two or three weeks for a new test.

Segregation Units

Once you've been sentenced by a disciplinary board or hearing officer to segregation time, you'll generally be taken straight from the hearing (in handcuffs) to the segregation unit. Occasionally, they may take you back to your cage to let you pack your belongings, or, if segregation is full, leave you in your cage until a segregation cell becomes available.

If you have a serious write-up and your fellow cons give the view that you're going to disciplinary segregation, then you might as will pack some things beforehand. But remember, segregation is punishment — this is the hole! You may not be able to smoke, drink coffee, get dope, have your books, etc., depending on the degree of severity of that particular segregation unit. Some prisons have more than one segregation unit.

That means you'll have to be creative in finding ways to bring these things into segregation with you. Meanwhile, your stuff will be taken to the hole with you, searched, inventoried and stored, and a few of the permitted items will be given to you. Once again, this varies. You might be able to have as many as six books, all your mail, legal work, even a change of clothes. You might not get anything.

Personal mail and legal work is often not too thoroughly searched. If you're allowed any cosmetic items, then powder bottles are good — dump out the powder, put your stuff at the bottom, then pour it back in. If you're storing tobacco this way, it's going to make it taste bad unless you wrap it in plastic first.

Some joints make you take your mattress with you wherever you go — making an excellent sort of prison backpack for lots of things you can sew inside. You can swallow smaller things (like a handcuff key) and of course there's the old "keistering" method of shoving something up your ass. Some guys view this as unmanly, but it can hardly be beaten as a great hiding place.

Generally your stuff is not going to be scrutinized that carefully, so items like razor blades, pieces of mirror (used as "peep" mirrors to see up and down the ranges), lighters, and other forbidden things will make it through. It's best to hide as much of this stuff in your belongings as possible so as much as possible makes it through.

When you arrive on a segregation unit, you'll be stripped, searched and taken to a cage. This will be your home until you go back to the main population; that means your old cell is history. That can really be too bad if you've invested a lot of time, effort, and money into fixing it up with shelves, cabinets, etc., or even if you just had a nice cell with no leaks and a working toilet. Once your time in segregation is up, you start out at the bottom again.

Segregation units house those who can't or won't go along with the program... most are more violent and vicious than the common prisoner. Once you get there, if you're a new guy in the joint you can most definitely expect the sex games to be brought to you ... even where movement is restricted. It is surprising how men can find ways to move around a cellblock that's supposedly locked down. Segregation units are kind of "rough and tumble," and stabbings and fights are regular occurrences there, so you've got to stay on your toes even more than usual.

There's no rest for the weary in prison.

Segregation units can also be racially polarized, so try to get a feel for your environment right away and keep your ears open. Usually segregation prisoners are allowed to come out in small groups of no more than 10 guys for between thirty minutes and an hour a day to take showers or walk around the tier. That's it for "activities." You spend the rest of your time in your cage, trying to ignore all the screaming.

Regular cigarettes are rare here, but loose tobacco (as well as coffee and other items) is available for inflated prices. A styrofoam coffee cup (small) of tobacco goes for between $5 and $10! One cigarette costs a dollar. A lighter is worth five bucks. Of course anything that is accepted can be used as currency. Under no circumstances should you get into debt on a segregation unit! Segregation is very rough.

One tactic used by enemies fighting with each other is "shit slinging." Prisoners make "bombs" by mixing feces, piss, spoiled milk and anything else that's foul and ripe for such a concoction, then letting it sit and fester for a few days or even weeks. Styrofoam cups with lids, or shampoo bottles, are typical receptacles. Then the bomb-maker uses his weapon to "gun down" his victim. A few guys at once will attack one prisoner, and not only the person, but his whole drum, will be hit with this shit. When he comes out at recreation, he's going to return the favor. This sort of fun and folly should be avoided, to say the least.

Welchers and snitches often "check-in" for protective custody and are kept in the same place — segregation. Prisoners on protective custody will have tags on their cell doors designating them as having "separate Tees," meaning they won't be let out except while alone. Still, this hated brand of prisoner is in the same unit as the prison's fiercest cons, and he will usually be "gunned down" with regularity. And God help them if they ever get "mistakenly" let out with other prisoners.

Also in segregation are a handful of prisoners strenuously rebelling against the prison administration. They are trying to do anything to hassle and harass the guards and any other prisoncrat. They throw shit at the guards and attack them with knives should they get half a chance. Others file lawsuits and try to organize others to resist along with them and fight the administration instead of throwing "bombs" at each other.

This "revolutionary" type of prisoner can be a source of some positive experiences since they will be glad to hold dialogues, debate and otherwise hold open discussions about the prison system, U.S. imperialism, world revolution and so on. These politically-aware prisoners are also on their way out of segregation to more secure facilities if they ever become at all successful in converting fellow cons. But it can take a while before this, and until then, these are the prisoners who might give you some hope. They have access to books and newspapers, which they will lend you. They encourage others to file lawsuits against the system as a whole for denying basic rights (as opposed to complaining about being busted with wine!) and will help anyone seeking relief from mistreatment by guards or the system.

Favors like this don't fall into the same category as other favors in prison. You don't "owe" anything back.

If petitions are passed around or demonstrations made, seriously consider participating — especially if you've got a long stretch in the hole. In the end, these are the only actions that have ever brought change to prison. Prisoncrats are very aware of this, which is why they discourage any political activity and look the other way at interracial feces-fights that merely waste the prisoners' energies and distract them from their common enemy.

If this reads a little like a political tract, that's because prisons are very political places. People are normally sent there for political reasons. The majority of prisoners have not committed a violent crime at all. They are doing time for the victimless crime of drug possession — a political offense. Prisons themselves are built as a result of political promises both to voters and to the people of impoverished rural counties who see a new prison as a source of income.

Perception of crime is normally used to galvanize the masses, often to distract them from real problems. No doubt, fear of crime is a galvanizing force, but it is also a neat tool to exculpate whoever is in charge (the ruling party) from any political shortcomings. Political life demands an excuse and that excuse is crime. Crime demands some people be sacrificed, and this will always be the person with the least political clout. The War on Drugs has served the ruling class for a long, long time to excuse falling standards of living and to instill fear and obedience into the masses. It has been going on so long, our prisons are full.

When the War on Drugs has captured as many malcontents as it can, then the focus will shift to someone else and they will become the new prisoners.

It is impossible to separate politics from prisons. Their very existence is political!

So to become involved in politics as a prisoner is only natural, although strongly discouraged by any prison administration.

At the same time, failure to awaken to the reality of the political reasons you are in prison, and even more so why you're in the hole, might be seen as awfully suspect behavior by others in segregation who are trying to unite the resistance. Although you should not participate in a protest you genuinely feel is wrong for some reason (and you should be man enough to say so), it is considered really wrong to not get involved in a demonstration just because the immediate issue doesn't concern you. This kind of behavior will get you ostracized, shunned and even attacked.

Certainly if you do not stand up with the other prisoners against the pigs, you cannot expect to get any help if the guards ever turn on you or you start to get brutalized by the same system that brutalizes you all.

Like it or not, you are one of "them" now, and you are expected to show some solidarity or come up with a different plan of action and be willing to follow up on it. It's fine to refuse to participate in certain forms of "protest" — slinging shit at guards for instance — in favor of more positive actions like lawsuits. Just know that you're expected to do something. By the way, shit-slinging, while satisfying in many ways, only serves to piss off the pigs even more, and can even result in an outside felony case against you, to no real purpose.

Pigs on segregation will be very petty, childish, violent and brutal with you if you "get out of line." The egregious violations of human rights that occur in U.S. prisons occur mostly on these segregation units. This is the place the pigs will hold you down and kick the shit out of you, blind you, deliberately break bones and crack skulls. Any resistance is met with what can only be described as torture. In fact, in commenting on a 1992 case, Supreme Court Justice (!) Harry A. Blackmun wrote that:

> "...various kinds of state-sponsored torture and abuse — of the kind ingeniously designed to cause pain... lashing prisoners with leather straps, whipping them with rubber hoses, beating them with naked fists, shocking them with electric currents, asphyxiating them short of death, intentionally exposing them to undue heat or cold, or forcibly injecting them with psychosis-inducing drugs... techniques commonly thought to be practiced only outside this nation's borders, are hardly unknown within this nation's prisons."

Most of these sorts of tortures and abuses go on in segregation, where the most thuggish and repulsive of pigs work — often because they are not tolerated in the mainline, even by other guards. This sort of "guard" will do all he can to violate your rights and find a pretext to deny you your meager privileges on the segregation unit. He does this precisely so that eventually someone will break and react ("go off" in prison terminology). Once a prisoner goes off, the goon squad is called in and they attack each prisoner, cell by cell, with dogs, water hoses, gas, truncheons, sticks, the works. Wearing helmets, kneepads and other body armor these guys charge into each cell and thoroughly beat the prisoner, often cuffing him and trussing him up first.

This mayhem, really impossible to describe adequately, can go on hour after hour and even day after day. News of this may never reach the outside world, but when and if it does, it is not believed and not reported. This is true even if men are beaten to death during such episodes.

Here, in the bottom rung of hell, you have no advocate but yourself. The stultifying violence you will experience here at the hands of guards is a truly pathetic sight. If you've ever watched a man mercilessly beat a chained dog, and listened to the yelps and squeals of pain, you have an idea of what goes on in prison segregation units.

God help you.

Your Rights

Going to prison doesn't mean you lose all your rights — though prison officials may try to convince you otherwise — but you've got to fight for them all by your lonesome.

Your rights fall into two categories: those emanating from the U.S. Constitution and those created by state law (called "state-created liberty interests"). In a nutshell you have the right to:

1. Be free from cruel and unusual punishment (8th Amendment). This covers not only freedom from beatings but should ensure adequate food, medical care and living conditions considered fit for humans. The simple filth of most prisons makes them cruel and unusual for this reason alone. You also have a right to meaningful and adequate recreation.

2. To have access to the courts (6th Amendment). This means you have a right to prepare and file legal documents without limitation or restriction by your captors, to have confidential access to and from the courts and attorneys. Legal mail, for instance, sent by you or delivered to you must remain sealed, although it can be searched in your presence prior to your getting it. You have a right to access legal materials and books (like a law library) and free paper, pens,

envelopes, photocopying, and postage for all your legal work if you have less than a certain amount of money in your account. This varies from prison to prison but is usually around $20 or $30. In preparing your legal documents — be they issues dealing with your case, a case against the prison system and its conditions, or anything else going to the courts — you have a right to get help from a jailhouse lawyer. A jailhouse lawyer can be any prisoner who has learned some law. In other words, the prison administration cannot stop someone from helping you.

Jailhouse lawyers, by the way, can be of far more use than "real" attorneys on the outside. Prisoner advocates are often more dedicated, creative and have studied the law a lot more than their counterparts in the free world.

3. To practice your religion (1st Amendment). You have the right to hold any belief and not be forced to hold nor attend any services of any faith. You are allowed to receive and possess your holy book and other religious materials, wear your faith's medallion or headgear (like skull caps), and to have a diet prescribed by your religion. So Jews and Muslims must be given an alternative to pork and some kinds of Buddhists must have access to nutritious vegetarian fare. Also, you can let your beard or hair grow if that is part of your faith, and you are allowed to attend worship services and be visited by a chaplain/imam or other religious "clergyman" if you desire. Any restriction or limitation the state wants to impose out of legitimate security concerns has to apply equally to all religions.

In practice, non-Christian religions, particularly Muslims, catch a lot of flack from state prisons, which are often the domain of "Christo-fascists." The federal system is far more advanced in this respect than are the state systems.

4. You have the right to be free from discrimination based on race, gender, religion, etc. (14th Amendment) which means basically that. It also means you cannot be treated differently from other, similarly confined prisoners in your particular joint.

5. You have a right to due process (14th Amendment). They're not allowed to punish you without "due process" of law, nor can any state-created liberty interest be taken from you without some kind of trial. As we've seen before, prison due process boils down to the

right to a hearing and to challenge any accusation before they punish you.

6. You have a right to free speech, free access to the press, and to public information (1st Amendment). That means you can write to whomever you want to (unless he or she is also a prisoner). You can use any language you want. Likewise, anyone (who is not also a prisoner) can write to you. You may receive books, magazines, papers, etc. without restriction save for legitimate security concerns. So you don't have a right to have bomb-making instructions or the like. You're allowed to write whatever you want and to keep whatever you write. You can have confidential correspondence with representatives.

Of course all mail — incoming and outgoing — is subject to search, and prison authorities can confiscate your outgoing mail if they suspect it contains criminal plans, etc. Prisons usually give everyone around 10 pre-stamped envelopes each month to facilitate this right to write, and prisons must supply free writing paper and pens to any who request it.

You've got more rights, these are just the big ones. More help can be obtained through some of the contacts in the Appendix or from sources within your particular prison.

You do not have a constitutional right to visits, to phone calls, a prison job, education (vocational or otherwise), and of course, you're not free from searches and cell shakedowns at any time. You don't have any right to live in any certain cell or any certain prison, and your captors are permitted to transfer you at any time to another facility.

You also have no right to commissary, radio, TV, or tape recorders/players. These can be granted to you under state statute and if they are, then they've got to run you through a little trial before they can take them away from you. Also, if some sort of privilege is allowed some, it must be equally available to others who are similarly-situated. To find out your rights under state statute, look in a state statute book under "Corrections" or "Prisons" and then find a section called "Rights of Prisoners" (or something similar). Here's where all your state-created liberty interests are spelled out.

Violations of state-created liberty interests are violations of state law. Moreover, if they've been violated without due process, there is also a violation of federal law (the constitutionally protected right to due process) and a violation of your civil rights.

Marionization

Having these rights in theory doesn't guarantee them in practice, and prison officials hardly go out of their way to extend them to you or even tell you about them. In fact, across the country in both state and federal facilities, prisons are embracing a process that has come to be known as "Marionization" after the permanently locked-down maximum control unit prison in Marion, IL (mentioned earlier).

With "Marionization," rights of prisoners are being actively and vigorously stripped away to the point that the treatment of U.S. prisoners now constitutes not only gross violation of American constitutional rights, but of generally accepted human rights as espoused by such organizations as the United Nations and its Standard Minimum Rules for the Treatment of Prisoners.

It's the kind of thing politicians like to point out about Iraq or the old Soviet Gulag System. They never mention the number of U.S. prisons in the same category.

The majority of state prisons in the United States have already been found in violation of the 8th Amendment's prohibition against "cruel and unusual punishments" and are under court order to improve.

Of course, if a prison's conditions break the law, what are they gonna do — send it to jail? Haw haw haw. But it's not that funny when you have to live in a place that is so repugnant that judges across the country are ordering them to conform to the law or else.

And, as we know, there is no "or else." The logical thing to do would be to order a prison to be shut down until it can come up to constitutional minimums, but if that were done, most state prisons would have to be closed. We can't have that.

So state prisons, though violating the Constitution, continue to operate under what are known as "consent decrees." Basically, the state admits the prison is a hell-hole and promises to start cleaning things up. There isn't much anyone will do to enforce the law, so they remain overcrowded and disease-ridden.

No federal prison, by the way, is in violation of the Constitution. Federal prisons are known to be generally "better" than state prisons. But with Marionization, all prisons will soon be equal — equally harsh.

Marionization essentially means the gradual but continual removal of a prisoner's rights, mainly by such gimmicks as declaring "lock-downs" of increasing duration. During lockdowns, normal prison life is suspended and everybody is kept in their cells while guards secure the prison. Lockdowns are normally employed after prison authorities have lost control, as in a riot. They are also used to "freeze" things into place while investigating a murder or a series of on-going crimes. For instance, if the warden feels there are too many weapons showing up, he may have the place locked down so that each cell can be searched and all weapons confiscated.

Lockdowns can last as long as a week — or at least they used to last that long. Now it is common for prisons to go on lockdown for months at a time. Marion opened in 1963, went on lockdown in 1983 and has been there ever since. Lockdown — the strict control of the whole prison's population — has become the *de facto* normal operating status at Marion. No one talks about when that lockdown will end.

Central to Marionization is the denial of rights to all prisoners equally. This skirts a lot of the issues of equal protection under the Constitution as well as the state-created liberty interests that must be extended to all prisoners at a facility. In other words, phone or visitation privileges are taken away from every prisoner by a lockdown order, and, since the lockdown never ends, the rights don't come back.

Buried Alive

New prisons open up without the problem of established rights. They just don't institute them in the first place. As for constitutional rights, these, too, are ignored and with such measures as no visits, etc., the outside world — if it gave a shit — can't hear about it. It's not in the news and the ACLU doesn't even get involved. Support groups from outside have no way to penetrate the prison, and news organizations have never found suffering prisoners to be any good for selling advertising. The world forgets...

Once a prison gets to this type of red-alert status, further repression is easy. If anyone so much as dares throw food at a guard, the inmate can be punished in ways that seem inhumane at best. A prisoner who refuses any order from a guard can be immediately punished.

But what are you gonna do with a guy who's already in prison within a prison? Throw him in prison? Haw haw haw.

What they do is strip the guy naked and chain him by all four limbs and his neck to the bed and leave him like that for 24 hours. Then another 24, then another, until he gets his mind right. If he resists even a little bit, he is beaten to a pulp and then chained to the steel bed.

Of course with no outside scrutiny in the slightest, it's easy to see how abuses might occur. And they do.

Grievances

As an individual in prison you need to not only be aware of your rights but also to protect them, to see to it that those rights are respected. At least you have to know how to strike back if they are violated. Otherwise, the abuse will only get worse. Perhaps even more horrifying is the thought that you may come to see it as normal, even "fair," treatment.

The most effective way to confront the infringement of your rights as an individual is through lawsuits. Lawsuits are a super pain-in-the-ass for prisoncrats, not to mention costly affairs for them to litigate. It usually doesn't cost you a dime, it only requires a little time and effort.

Any time your rights are violated, or if you are made to obey an intolerable policy, and especially if you have any hope of improving prison life in the tiniest way (the only way, unfortunately!), you have got to file a grievance first.

You should have gotten a copy of the grievance policy during orientation along with your rule book. Familiarize yourself with it. Get copies of grievance forms by sending a request slip to the cell house or dorm counselor. Usually you must file them within something like 2 or 3 days of an incident, so it's a good idea to have these forms on hand in advance.

Let's say you broke your arm and a guard refused to let you go to the infirmary (this is a very typical situation). First, get the pig's name. Try to contact any other pig (saving names all the time). If all else fails, when the pill-pusher (nurse, med-tech) comes by on the daily "pill-run," show him your broken arm and complain about it. Get his name. Perhaps someone eventually relents and lets you sign up for sick call, and a few days later you get to see a doctor, who X-rays the arm and sends you to an outside hospital to have your broken arm set.

As soon as you return to prison, or to your cell, file a grievance. The two- or three-day delay was cruel and unusual; you want monetary compensation, and you want the pigs and the med-tech fired. Ask for whatever you want, because there's no chance of you getting any relief so early in the game.

Why do this if it's not going to pay off? Because this is the first step. You've got to exhaust all your remedies prior to moving up the ladder and getting the thing in court. If you forget, you might get out of it by claiming you filed a grievance but now it's been conveniently "lost." But it is best to really file one. You have two years to file a lawsuit from the time your rights are violated.

The grievance will go to an "investigator" who will talk to you, the pigs and the med-tech and then write up a report and send it to the grievance committee to hear. Then you'll be called before the committee to state your case and they will tell you you're an idiot and then you tell them you want it to go to the next level. That's the warden.

The warden will agree wholeheartedly with the committee's conclusion that you're an idiot and nothing bad happened. Now you take all this and send it "downstate" to the Commissioner/Department of Corrections (DOC) central office. They, too, will deny your claim. Surprise!

And now you can sue. This process of getting rejected might eat up a month or two, but it's got to be done. If it is unduly held up any longer, you start hounding the investigator with inquiries about why your case is taking too long, and, of course, you might even file a grievance!

Always keep carbon copies of all letters.

If things take too long, you should write the warden, the DOC, everybody. This will help you later on to show you've been diligent, etc. It's possible to fake these letters by back-dating them and keeping only a carbon, but under the circumstances, it's a lot better to really write the letters.

Filing A Lawsuit

It's part of the popular Rush Limbaugh mythology that prisoners waste honest taxpayers' money filing "frivolous lawsuits." Media stories of prisoners suing wardens for giving them creamy-style peanut butter instead of the crunchy-style they ordered are easy to find. But this view of prisoners' litigation doesn't seriously look at why this happens. You're just supposed to make the judgment that these imprisoned scum are even less deserving of pity than you already thought.

Of course, these stories are also easy for the media to do, as prisoncrats are more than happy to assist "journalists" who make prisoners more hated in society. This can only help them isolate prisoners and deflect criticism when authorities are exposed committing atrocities.

Maybe even you, the person reading this book, might think lawsuits and all this information about filing grievances is not information you truly need to prepare for prison. But if you manage to survive the first few months without being killed or transformed into a raving nut-case, this is a skill you must master or face even more problems behind bars.

In the free world, if the store sells you the wrong thing, you can easily take it back and complain to get your money back or get the right thing. If one store employee fails to help you, you can go to his/her boss and on up the line.

In prison, you may have no other recourse to being ripped off except to file a lawsuit. That seems ridiculous and it is. But the fact of the situation is, the kindly guards or fellow cons around you don't care one whit about you — they don't care if you live or die, if you're in pain or not. They certainly don't care if someone shorted you at the commissary.

So the same methods are used to redress everything. If they beat the shit out of you and knock out all your teeth: file a lawsuit. If they give you the wrong kind of peanut butter: file a lawsuit. By the time it happens to you, you may be sufficiently tormented that you'd kill somebody over a jar of peanut butter, so filing a lawsuit is no big deal.

The Paperwork

First you need to get the proper forms for filing suit and to find out exactly what rights of yours were violated, so you can talk that talk. Otherwise the suit will just come back to you.

The forms can be had from the prison law library or by writing the local U.S. District Court and requesting them (they're free!). The Appendix lists "self-help" litigation manuals and Lewisburg Legal Bulletins — get the bulletins which you need, since they are very thorough, and if you can't afford a litigation manual, they can suffice. You may also be able to buy one through a contact on the outside or borrow one from another prisoner or, best, the prison library.

Fill out the forms. Put down all the pigs and the medical technician as "Defendants." Under "causes of action" you would state in the space provided just exactly what rights were violated; what they did wrong. And you need to cite it. For example, in this case, you would state, "Defendants, et al., by denying Plaintiff medical attention for a broken arm for two days, violated his right to be free from cruel and unusual punishment; 8th U.S. Const. Amendment."

Under the "Facts" portion of the form you tell what happened — in the order that it happened. Be as precise as possible and don't go off on any tirades or start talking about things that are not pertinent ("the guard, Officer X, hates my guts because he's a Klansman..."). After you describe what happened, you sum up that "each Defendant, in their individual and official capacities, intentionally disregarded Plaintiff's rights and were willfully negligent in denying him timely medical attention." Under the part that says, "Damage/Relief," you ask for:

1. Declaratory relief that Defendants have violated Plaintiff's rights as alleged.
2. Injunctive relief barring them from retaliation for having filed this suit.
3. Actual damages in compensation for suffering, pain, trauma, and mental stress as a result of being denied treatment for a broken arm for two days in the sum of $ (You Name It!) from each defendant respectively.
4. Punitive damages in the sum of $ (You Name It!) from each defendant respectively for their intentional and willful disregard of Plaintiff's rights, and the damages incurred thereby.
5. That the issues of your action be tried by jury trial.

Now you sign this thing and send in two copies for the court; one for each defendant, and one for the clerk to file, stamp and return to you. When you get your complaint forms also ask for enough "marshal service forms" so that you have one for each defendant and two copies of the "summons" for each defendant. Fill these out, and, along with your *pro forma pauperis* forms (showing you're too poor to pay for any of this), send it all to the clerk, asking that the enclosed (make a list) be filed.

Once filed, it will be served on all defendants, and usually within a month the Attorney General will file an "answer" to your complaint. You must reply to that accordingly. That answer along with everything else that comes after it, is far too complicated and far too important to explain here. This information can be gleaned from the bulletins, a lawyer, or other sources. Keep in mind that there are different clocks ticking on everything you do and you must be sure to make all deadlines and file everything within the time limits.

Because trials are costly and a pain for anyone, including the state, they will often offer you a deal at some point after they see you're serious and capable of going through with this. They will want to settle out of court, and, once again, such deals are too complex and variable to talk about here. Advice can come from lawyers, jailhouse lawyers, cons in the law library. Get as many opinions as you can.

The broken arm in this hypothetical case might get you an offer of $7,000 -$12,000. At trial you might get a hell of a lot more, but then again, that's a lot more work and you might get nothing. So take the offer into careful consideration.

Of course, trials can be appealed by the loser, whether that's you or the state. This makes lots more work for everyone and can drag things out for years.

Suits can also be used to challenge the oppressive conditions you live under, to challenge collective punishments or other larger rights issues. Some of these suits have done a lot to improve the plight of prisoners in general, and many have set precedents. They're important because, though they may not benefit you specifically, or benefit you very much (if at all), they help create legal groundwork for the other struggling crabs in the prison barrel, and might help someone just like you in the future.

Going down this road can be rewarding, but you need to hit the books because in these cases you're striking back at the system where they are forced to fight back and you have got to know what you're doing. An excellent and up-to-date publication on prisoners' rights and litigation is the *Prison Legal News* (P.O. Box 1684, Lake Worth, FL 33460. Subscriptions are $12/year. For prisoners, it's whatever you can spare; libraries and organizations pay $35 a year). This monthly is a compendium of articles written by some of the country's best jailhouse lawyers, and is a "must" for anyone trying to keep up with the prison litigation scene.

Of course, whenever you start filing grievances or lawsuits you can expect to be harassed by the prisoncrats. This goes with the territory, so be alert for this right away and consider it before going down this road. Make sure your suit isn't "frivolous" to you. You can protect yourself from retaliation by staying in contact with outside prisoners'-rights organizations and like-minded activists who can and will put pressure on the authorities and let them know somebody is watching. This won't stop them from spitting in your food, but it can curtail some of the more blatant antics.

5
Execution

The Death Penalty

If you don't get life, the next worst thing the state can do to you is kill you. This is arguably more merciful — far more merciful — than life imprisonment, but people tend to cling to their lives with all their might when they are truly threatened. If you get the death penalty, your life is definitely threatened.

One thing about the death penalty is you're not likely to become lost in the system anymore — after the state hands you a death sentence, they aren't going to accidentally let you out or consider you for work release or conjugal visits or anything else. If you get the death penalty the state is going to kill you.

Make no mistake about it. The death penalty means they kill you. The popular perception that death row prisoners are even more mollycoddled than the rest of prison population is fiction. And this fiction has made the path between courtroom and electric chair much faster over the years as laws are enacted to cut a prisoner's access to appeals — appeals the public thinks are a waste of time.

There is no reason to outline the arguments for or against the death penalty here. Most states have it. It exists. Likewise, any discussion about whether or not the death penalty is fairly applied is futile here. There are very few cases where the death penalty is applied in a "fair" manner. Indeed, this book is predicated on the notion that the whole "justice system" is capricious and abusive. That goes for a traffic ticket. It goes for capital crimes.

By the way, the various "crime bills" currently under consideration in the U.S. Congress all add an astonishing number of new crimes calling for the death penalty. In every version there are some that do not require that anyone lose their life or even get hurt. One of my favorites is the death penalty for anyone setting fire to government property. Which version will become our new law of the land remains to be seen as of this writing. But they've already picked the site for the new federal death house — Terre Haute, Indiana.

Why You Got The Death Penalty

Unless you have been convicted of serial murder in which you also mutilated your victims and slept with severed body parts, you could just as easily have drawn a life sentence, or just a few years, had it not been for a number of factors well outside your control. The judge, the community in which you are tried, the weather — they all come into play.

If the prosecutor is up for re-election or some other political force comes into the picture, a second-degree murder charge can easily become capital murder. But if you're looking at this part of the book from Death Row, there's no need to run through all the reasons you're there.

Probably you're poor. Probably you're uneducated. Certainly you are without any political or social connections.

Just how someone gets condemned to death is relatively unimportant here. In the end, the death penalty is a red herring. There are fewer than 3,000 people waiting to be killed by various states in the whole U.S. Then there are those other one million, three hundred thousand people locked up with them — many for incredibly long periods of time. To discuss whether or not the death penalty is "fair" or "humane" is really pretty sick to the extent that it ignores the plight of the rest of the prison population.

But it's a sexy issue and it does deflect public attention away from other, more pressing, issues.

Of course, the issue is very pressing should you be the one receiving a death sentence, so let's start there.

Going To The Death Chamber

Statistically, you've committed murder. That didn't used to be the case. Most people who've gotten the death penalty in the U.S. have been executed for rape. No state imposes the death penalty for rape anymore, but the federal government has managed to dream up capital crimes that don't include killing someone. At one time in the late '50s it became a capital offense to sell heroin to a minor. Things seem to be headed that way again, so maybe you didn't kill anyone.

It was probably a run-of-the-mill murder, but you got singled out for this. There is also a distinct possibility that you are innocent. Many people have been released from Death Row when they were able to prove their innocence at one of those time-wasting appeals the public has done away with.

Which brings us to the central point again. If you get a death sentence, the odds are you will fight it for an average of eight years and then be put to death. It could happen faster (but it'll take at least a year or two even if you beg them to kill you), and it could happen more slowly. Just don't count on any more than 15 years.

On Death Row you have the same objective as you've had since the cop first asked to see some ID: you need to get away from these people, you need to lessen the pain. If you don't manage to get off Death Row, the state will kill you. If you get off Death Row, you'll either go free or you'll go back to the main prison population — probably for life. Most of what happens now is way beyond your control. You control almost nothing now and are dependent on your lawyer and other people with specialized knowledge of your predicament.

This is not to suggest there's nothing you can do at this point — it's just that it's a very complex legal and political matter, too complex to be covered here. You might be one in a million who gets some kind of *60 Minutes* attention and somehow gets let go, but that is very, very unlikely. In fact, even if *60 Minutes* shows up, they aren't going to help you at all. They care only about ratings, and impending death interests them more than anything else. You can pray for that miracle — that outsider with stamina and clout pleading your case before the American public — but still, they'll probably kill you.

If you're on Death Row, they are going to kill you. There's not much you can do about that. Have I made this point clear?

What You Can Do

Of course, right up to the instant you're put to death there are some things you can do to reduce the pain and increase your likelihood of escaping or mitigating the punishment.

The first thing you must do is write everybody in the world and ask for help. Do anything you can to get a good lawyer who knows death-penalty law and is committed to helping you live. Although legislatures have begun to remove "obstacles" to carrying out the death sentence, filing the proper motions in the proper order and at the proper time can buy you years of time. All the guys on Death Row who aren't profoundly retarded will know some of these things. In many cases, appeals will be filed for you whether you want them or not.

So make sure you're following the very narrow path of appeals, and you can buy yourself a few more years. As long as you're alive, there's hope. Death sentences can be overturned or commuted. But you've got to get in line for this. Unless you fight, the state is going to kill you as fast as they can.

So one piece of advice that comes to mind is to try to have your case tried in a jurisdiction where there is no death penalty. Get tried in a state that won't impose it, or get tried by the federal government (at least before the new crime bill goes into effect and Terre Haute gets revved up). Or else see if you can be extradited to another state where you'll receive a longer (non-lethal) sentence. That way you may face 20 years in one state and the death penalty in another. Of course, if you should finish your sentence, or have parole forced on you, you'll be dragged back to the death state, but a lot can happen in 20 years. You could even escape.

If you escape, make it to a country that's reluctant to extradite anyone facing the death penalty. Germany is one of those countries, and so is Canada (although Canada is not reliable in this respect). For more information on this, see the part of the book on extradition.

Death Row

In nearly every state, Death Row prisoners are segregated from the main population and kept under much tighter security than anyone else. You get a single cell, meals are brought to you (sometimes a Death Row has its own kitchen and staff), not that the quality of the food will improve. Your visiting hours are more restricted and you get watched at all times by the guards.

In some states, like Florida, the term "Death Row" is a misnomer and it has been suggested that since the population of Florida's Death Row exceeds the population of a lot of incorporated villages in that state, it should be called "Death Town." In cases like this, a whole section of a prison may be dedicated to housing the men the state intends to kill.

Women slated for death are generally kept at a women's prison and then driven to the execution site a few days before or even on the day of their killing. Florida women waiting to "ride the lightening" are housed in a fairly small "community corrections"-type facility down south among the palm trees and not far from the beach. When it's time to kill them, they chain them up on an un-airconditioned bus and drive them north to Starke. No smoking on the bus, please.

This is the beginning of the "deathwatch," the crucial time when a prisoner is removed from his normal cell and surroundings and brought to another cell situated right next to the death chamber. He stays there in solitary, often listening intently as prison technicians laboriously practice each step in the "death protocol." These "protocols" are the choreographed instructions modern penologists have found are so essential to a "humane" execution.

Part of it includes testing and retesting the equipment to be used to kill the man in the next room. He can hear trap doors being sprung and adjusted. He can hear a tub of water sizzle and watch the lights dim as the chair is calibrated so that the correct amount of current will crackle through his body on the fateful day.

Most of what is known about the "protocol" comes from prisoners who have gone through it and then been reprieved with as little as an hour (or even less) before they are scheduled to die. The protocol is otherwise secret and is being revised all the time, as each execution suggests minor changes to the prison staff.

The protocol is mostly designed to calm the prison staff. Each person connected with the killing has a set of tasks to perform and understands he is but one part of the entire process. This helps to alleviate any feelings of guilt or confusion and lets the staff reply to any "how could you do this?" questions by answering, more or less, that they didn't do anything but their little part of the job.

And they are right, too. The state (and the population's consent) has brought this about. Of course, the guy who straps the prisoner into the chair plays a very significant role, but the protocol, coupled with the fact that many prisons only allow volunteers to take part in this macabre ritual, helps ease his mind. And there is every indication it works.

The protocol also is supposed to help the prisoner remain calm by making him feel a part of the whole procedure and instilling confidence that his killing is going to be carried out by competent people.

Avoiding chaos and surprises of any kind is of paramount importance.

Hence the holding cell next to the killing machine, where the prisoner spends the last day or few days of his life. By the rule-books, the prisoners are not supposed to be brought to this cell until the day before the execution. In reality, they are sometimes brought here as much as a week early. In some cases a prisoner is tricked into leaving his cell under some pretext and never returns to his old cell. His belongings are gathered up and brought to him (leaving out those things about-to-die prisoners aren't allowed to have), and he's locked up in the holding cell.

This is known as "kidnapping" among death row prisoners. It's done to prevent any aberrations, such as a combative prisoner, or one who makes preparations to commit suicide at the last possible moment.

Here, in the holding cell, the prisoner is physically watched 24 hours a day. This is done partially to prevent him from "cheating the hangman" and committing suicide, and partially for unknown reasons. On the last day of his life a prisoner can expect to share a cell with a guard who records each and every thing the prisoner does, no matter how minute.

Many prisoners report that — contrary to what you might think — they sleep very peacefully while in this death cell. Perhaps it is a feeling of relief after all these years of resisting the inevitable.

Visiting rules are relaxed to varying degrees, and certain privileges are extended to the condemned man. He can have just about whatever he wants from the commissary, he can order up and watch videos with the guards. At times, female visitation rules against too much contact or kissing are relaxed to the point that some condemned men have managed to even get laid before they die.

A lot of this sort of thing is done out of pity by the guards, who, no matter how much they might believe in their jobs, find it cruel and unusual to deny a man one last piece of ass before his death.

Media restrictions, too, are relaxed. So prisoners can give interviews until just a few hours before they are scheduled to die.

Often, on his last day, a condemned man's cell is full of a couple of relatives, a guard, and maybe a wife or girlfriend, all drinking commissary soft drinks and eating junk food while trying to maintain their composure. Most don't. Someone is always crying.

Prisoners have described this as being especially tough on them. On the one hand, they don't want to deny their families these last few moments with them, and on the other, seeing the intense emotional pain of loved ones is too much. He wants to comfort them, but, understandably, finds he has little strength left to do it. The strain of preparing to die is now mixed with the strain of seeing the suffering of family members and the knowledge that it's all his fault.

The scene is not pretty. When one prisoner was being visited by his family and some guards came to get him, his little girl grabbed his leg tightly, wailing, "Don't kill my Daddy!"

Now all visitors and media are made to leave the prisoner early in the evening of the night of the execution. *De facto* understandings have sprung up between Death Row prisoners and their captors to make things easier. For instance, in return for an inmate's promise not to fight or struggle when it's time to walk the last mile, prison authorities agree informally not to chain him. It is felt to be more dignified and manly for a guy to saunter to his death unfettered, rather than be trussed up and forced to drag his chains along the floor.

Some guys do fight, however, and this is dealt with the same as it is anywhere else in prison — the goon squad comes and beats the man into submission.

Largely to prevent this type of behavior and to ease the ordeal for the condemned man, it is now common to give sedatives to the prisoner at intervals in the last few hours. Injection is most common and the drug is usually Valium or Versed at about half the dose normally used for anesthesia.

The prisoner is free to reject the drugs, but they are strongly encouraged to take them, and most guys do.

The Last Hour, The Last Minutes

Most executions these days are scheduled for 12:01 on the morning of the day specified on the death warrant. This is to ensure the prison has use of the full 24-hour window it is allowed — something necessary, as courts can issue stays and reverse stays and otherwise hold up an execution until the last possible moment. Prison authorities want to get this thing done with, and so they are prepared to kill their prisoner at the first moment possible. If there is a flurry of appeals and they keep getting red and green lights, they are ready. With the man strapped into whatever contraption he's going to die in, they simply wait for the first moment they've got the green light and kill him. The issue may still be before some other court, but once the sentence is carried out, it's a moot point.

Prison officials and employees connected to the execution find it is a stressful experience at best, and the pressure of coming so close to doing the deed and then being ordered to stand down is remarkably depressing to them. As it is, people who participate in executions suffer a higher incidence of domestic and related problems as a result of their strange line of work.

Shortly before the killing, authorities typically lock the entire prison down as a safety precaution. Executions provoke strong reactions among the caged men, and all attention has to be focused on this one task. The lockdown lasts until the warden deems things to be settled down enough. This could be a few hours after the death, or even a couple of days. As another means of calming and distracting the rest of the population, prisons sometimes show pornographic videotapes — something guaranteed to catch at least some of their attention, and a privilege not otherwise available.

Last Requests

You don't get to wear your biker jacket to the chair. You don't get to wear anything special at all. You'll be executed in your prison uniform. You might get to have a picture of your wife next to your heart or something, but probably not. Generally, you won't be given an opportunity to choreograph your execution in any way that evokes symbolism (except to have a prison-approved religious-type there, moaning Bible verses).

Of course, you can subvert this to some extent with things you can blurt out to the onlookers, tattoos made for the occasion, or items secreted away in your clothing or body.

Yeah, they do stuff cotton or some other type of plug up your ass and a catheter device in your penis to deal with the body's involuntary evacuation of bodily fluids upon death. Sometimes this has been accomplished with a diaper. At least one design of electric chair includes a plexiglass seat with holes in it, so escaping fluids (including blood) can be captured in a pan underneath. After all, there will be witnesses to this event, and the state doesn't want to offend anyone.

As mentioned before, you're going to get to pretty much watch whatever videos you want, and presumably the same goes for reading material. Of course, you'll be unofficially allowed at least some heavy groping with your girlfriend or wife.

Drugs, too, though not officially on the menu, are available even in this supposedly securest of cells, and autopsies performed on executed men have shown them to have had recent access to alcohol, amphetamines and marijuana. Of course, there's also the tranquilizer they'll supply you with before they kill you.

And then there's the last meal.

Legend has it you can have anything you want, and newspapers like to make sure they detail the dead man's final meal. It's kind of like reading tea leaves or something, as if a review of a man's final repast will reveal some salient thing about his personality, or explain his crime, or unravel the mystery of death. The same attitude is taken toward "his last words."

The truth of the matter is, you can have whatever you want that the warden is willing to get for you. They might go all out and let you order something from a certain special restaurant, or they might just tell you what's fresh in the kitchen and see if you'll go for it.

As for last words, you're normally allowed to make some kind of a brief statement before they kill you. This may be in front of the execution witnesses and it may not be. You can say what you want, but don't expect to filibuster your way to a delayed execution. At some point they'll tell you to shut up and sit down. Coming up with something haunting or inflammatory might be fun (although you'll never see the results of it), but I think those guys who decline to say anything infuriate the hyena public more than anyone else. After all, here was their chance to get into the mind of a condemned man and he deprived them of it!

You are generally allowed to invite a few people to your execution, including other prisoners. They will join the rest of the mob pressing their noses against the glass of the death chamber or sitting quietly behind a curtain, waiting for the show to begin. The states all have different ways of handling this delicate problem, and almost always screen off the audience from the condemned man until the last minute, when they allow them to watch the killing. After that, they're screened off again and led away. Sometimes they have to sign a statement swearing they saw you die.

None of this matters to you, of course, since you're dead by this time.

At a hanging in Washington State in 1993, viewers were not permitted to see the killing, but were allowed to watch only the silhouette of the man falling through the trap door and bouncing back up a few feet with his neck broken. This was accomplished by using a thin cloth for a screen and bright back-lighting to give a sort of Hitchcockian feeling to the show.

Lethal Injection

This form of execution is becoming all the rage in a lot of states and it is performed in one of two ways, depending on whether you're in Texas or not.

In Texas, all the lethal chemicals are mixed into one big syringe and injected into the body. Furthermore, this is done by a man with no medical training save on-the-job experience killing people for the state. He often has to dig around and solicit the prisoner's help in finding a suitable vein.

The concept of step-by-step anesthetizing and gradually turning off various life functions has proved too much trouble for Texas. Hence, executed prisoners in Texas are more prone to roll around, gag, gasp for air, groan and buck and strain than their counterparts in, say, Nevada.

All the other states use a multi-part system, pouring one chemical after another into a large tube inserted into a large vein in the prisoner's body. Normally this is the arm, but some guys' arms have proven too full of collapsed veins and scar tissue, so it has been necessary to insert the tube into the groin. The neck, too, offers possibilities. Where possible, the tube is inserted toward the heart, not away (as it is in normal medical procedure). This helps a quicker onset of these already fast-acting drugs.

An already-sedated prisoner is strapped to a gurney hooked up to the machine and awaits the injections. In addition to the tranquilizing agent (which could be any of a number of things — Valium, Versed, and even a sub-anesthetic dose of sodium pentathol have been used), he's probably had an injection of an antihistamine to prevent allergic reactions and gagging. This antihistamine might be plain old Benadryl, or it may be hydroxyzine, an antihistamine commonly used as a pre-op for both its drying and its tranquilizing effects.

The first drug to hit the prisoner is 15cc of 2% sodium pentathol over a 10-second period. That knocks him out and begins to depress respiration. One minute later, 15cc of pancuronium is administered over another 10 seconds, followed by a one-minute wait. After that comes a hit of 15cc of potassium chloride which should stop the heart. Death follows within two minutes.

If done properly, this system should very quickly render the man or woman absolutely unconscious, halt breathing and begin to cause extensive brain damage well before the heartbeat is halted. Some states have experimented with a two-chemical solution based on a strong barbiturate to knock the person out and halt breathing while the potassium chloride stops the heart. Some medical experts have testified that it is possible that such people would experience painful suffocation but not be able to communicate this, because they are essentially paralyzed. Nobody has lived through it to tell.

Electrocution

This was introduced in New York City in 1889 as a more humane method of killing people than hanging. For some years, the governor had charged a task force with coming up with such a method, but one of the most humane and quick methods — the guillotine — was rejected as being too gruesome. Hence the electric chair.

Since then, the chair has been adopted by a majority of the states, and is still the preferred method in 12 states (lethal injection is in use in 22). In nearly every state where there is an electric chair it is referred to as "old Sparky" and is said to have been made from wood taken from the prison gallows. This last bit sounds like a nice anecdote but usually isn't true.

Electrocutions have been carried out extensively in the United States, and from the beginning it's been apparent something was wrong. Although seemingly preferable to hanging (which could result in a slow strangling death of the condemned or else rip his head off entirely), it has never seemed to be anything like "painless," let alone humane.

Typically, electrocuted people thrash around the chair in spasms, their skin burns to a crisp near the electrodes, and lesser burns occur throughout the body. Sometimes the clothing or the body itself catches fire.

Most disturbing is the frequency with which an electrocution fails, and jolt after painful jolt is required to kill the person. This happened in 1988 when a man strapped to the chair was electrocuted on and off for forty-five minutes before doctors could be sure he was dead. Well before that, sickened spectators were escorted from the room.

Part of the problem with electrocution is associated with the age and decrepitude of the electric chairs themselves. After hitting their height in the '30s and '40s, executions began to drop off, dwindling to just a few a year before the death penalty as written was declared unconstitutional by the Supreme Court in 1972. Although it was reinstated slowly, starting in 1976, it took a while for the states to build up their Death Rows and, by the time they got around to using them, the machinery was simply out of date.

One problem some states had was the size of the chair itself. Built to kill an average-sized man at the turn of the century, they were too small for today's healthier, burlier executee. Parts of the chairs made from leather had rotted or otherwise decayed. Electrodes were pitted and covered with mineral deposits, and couldn't transmit electricity well enough.

Added to that was the general lack of knowledge of just how electrocution works. As it turned out, no one had bothered to write any of this down, and sometimes the executioner would throw the switch and immediately blow out the transformer as well as not killing the prisoner (although he certainly got a non-lethal jolt). These and other problems have led to something of a renaissance in execution devices led by a man named Fred Leuchter.

Leuchter has designed and built electric chairs, lethal injection machines, and gallows. He steadfastly maintains that electrocution is the least painful way to go. It is the method he would choose, if he ever had to choose. But it's got to be done right.

Luckily, a lot of states have purchased new chairs or had their chairs refurbished by Fred, and these are the ones which work the best. Fred stands by his work, guarantees it unconditionally, and will even be on hand to help out in the event that the prison personnel (which he trains in a special seminar) are faced with a last-minute glitch. His chair at the death house in Tennessee bears a small plaque with his name and address on it. Fred's quality goes in before his name goes on!

According to Fred, the keys to a good electrocution are nice, tight and clean electrodes on both ankles as well as a good one on the head. Older electric chairs have just one electrode in through the head and another out through one foot. This electrocutes only half the body, he says, and is cruel.

A good electric chair also takes into account voltage, current, connections, duration and number of jolts. To ensure a good connection at each electrode, for instance, Fred insists on using sponges soaked in saline solution. This also minimizes the amount of superficial burns, or "cooking," of the body.

The amount and intensity of the electrical jolts have to be calibrated to cause maximum damage in minimum time. Done right, Fred says, unconsciousness can be achieved in 4.116 milliseconds. Death can occur in 1/240th of a second. To do this, Fred suggests two 2,600 volt jolts lasting one minute each, ten seconds apart. Although the first jolt will kill the man, Fred has theorized that it is just possible that the shock could cause the heart to spasm instead of seizing as it should. If that happens, there's the slim possibility that the guy could still be alive (albeit unconscious). A ten-second wait is to let the body's neuro-transmitters degrade to the point where that's not possible after the second jolt.

Anything else is likely to cause suffering. Loose electrodes not only encourage third-degree burns of the skin, they also markedly reduce the current flowing through a body to the point that all the electricity does is cause excruciating pain and not death. Low current might cause death, but if applied incorrectly or for too long can cause the flesh to literally cook to a point where it begins to fall off the bone. Taking a body out of an electric chair can be a grotesque experience, as the body begins to fall apart and boiled blood trickles from openings in the corpse.

Applications of electricity that are too weak may also have the effect of creating a human vegetable. South Carolina, for instance, at one time proposed killing Donald "Pee Wee" Gaskins using one big shock of 2,000 volts for five seconds, then a 1,000 volt jolt for eight seconds to be followed by a two minute jolt of 250 volts. Such a routine, according to Fred, could be disastrous. The first jolts might easily render him brain dead (maybe even dead dead). But the 250 volt shock might have the effect of restarting the poor bastard's heart and leave him very much alive in the chair.

So if you're going to the chair, make sure the state's got a genuine Fred Leuchter chair. Fred's motto is "Capital Punishment, not Capital Torture."

The Gas Chamber

This idea was cooked up by an army major in 1924 who, musing on the effects of poison gas in WWI, thought a more concentrated blast of gas would be even more humane than electrocution. It's debatable.

All the gas chambers in use in the U.S. today were built by Eaton Metal Products of Salt Lake City, and hundreds of people have been killed in them, so they do work. But they're not pleasant.

Since the State of California uses the gas chamber, lots of people are still facing it. It's also in use in another 4 states.

Fred Leuchter thinks they should only be used as a last resort, and would like to see them abolished. He says they're dangerous to the operators and spectators, and cruel to the guy trapped inside. You may take some comfort in that — if you're slated to die in a gas chamber you may be taking a pig or two with you! Unfortunately, flocks of birds may go down when the prison vents the poison gas through the exhaust pipe out the roof.

The routine for gas chamber death is the same for all of them. The prisoner is strapped into a chair over a bowl with a tube leading into it from the wall. Attached to the chair on a hook is a gauze bag containing about a pound of cyanide. A string leads from this hook to a hole in the wall, and out of the chamber. A stethoscope leads from the prisoner's heart to the wall, where it goes to the outside to a doctor who is listening for the heartbeat to stop. Another tube, coming from the outside, leads from the wall into the bowl, and it's through this that someone pours sulfuric acid (that alone smells pretty terrible, like rotten eggs).

When it's time to do the deed, the executioner pulls the string on the bag of cyanide, letting it drop into the sulfuric acid, and then the fun begins. It might take a few minutes for much of the lethal gas to creep up around the prisoner while onlookers gawk. Then the gas hits in earnest.

It is not fast. In 1967, when the government of California executed Aaron Mitchell, his head first dropped to his chest. Then he raised it up and looked toward one of the spectator windows (louvered so they could see him but not vice versa) and just stared. He sat that way for seven minutes, his chest heaving and saliva bubbling through his lips, then he tucked his thumbs into his fists and his head slumped forward to his chest again. He still wasn't dead, though. It took another five minutes before his heart stopped beating.

More recently, in 1983, a man named Jimmy Lee Grey was executed in Missouri's gas chamber (this one built by prison labor and not by the Utah company), and this provided another ghastly look at the "humane" gas chamber.

Witnesses to the execution said Grey struggled and convulsed for eight minutes, during which time he gasped 11 times. Then he started banging his head on a pole behind him and continued to struggle against the leather bonds. At that point officials started hustling the observers out of the room. Grey continued to bang his head, so one of the witnesses asked the warden on the way out if the man was dead. Warden Eddie Lucas replied, "Most definitely."

Missouri no longer uses its gas chamber, and, instead, has a lethal injection machine developed by Fred Leuchter.

Hanging

The chances of being hanged in the U.S. have declined rapidly until it looks like only certain prisoners condemned to death in Delaware have been "grandfathered in" to get the gallows while the rest of them get lethal injection. The guy who's slated to get the gallows may have insisted on his right to hang just to piss off the state, which had no gallows at the time and has been forced to build one at a cost of at least $80,000. Washington State and Montana give the condemned a choice between hanging and lethal injection.

So I won't spend a lot of time on it. Put it this way: it's killed a lot of people. Done correctly (and the only real experts on hanging left in the world come from South Africa), it can be very quick. Make sure your executioner is from South Africa.

Firing Squad

Well, this is how the military kills you and how you can be executed in Utah and Idaho. It's cheap and dirty. Although killing a guy with a bullet to the back of the head is a very fast and effective way of executing him (and is the method used in China), it's not the way it's done here.

In the U.S., the prisoner faces a squad of five men who are obscured by a slit-screen (and one of whom has a blank, of course) who are supposed to fire at a target pinned over the man's heart. The blank is supposed to let each man live with the fantasy that he was not the one to kill the guy. In fact, the guy with the blank knows he's the guy with the blank since his rifle won't have any recoil.

Although the method is intended to kill a person pretty quickly from massive trauma to the heart and chest cavity, the marksmen have a disturbing habit of aiming away from the heart and missing it altogether. Even in cases where the heart is obliterated, the condemned man is certain to linger on for at least another minute or minute and a half.

Cheating The Hangman

Now, if you want to fuck the system up, some ideas come to mind.

The first one is, of course, to kill yourself. This puts the matter into your hands, giving you just that much more control over your own life (and death). This way you won't have to play the state's game all the way down to them asking you if you have anything to say. (Notice how in this whole process so far they never really cared what you had to say? You can bet they don't now. It's just for the newspapers.)

To this end, the best way is to buy enough heroin, any barbiturate, or even a sedative, for an overdose. Make sure you've got plenty. Then put a plastic bag over your head or otherwise seal your mouth and nose (toilet paper and a couple of socks can do the trick). Nighty-night! Make sure to do this in such a way and place that you cannot be discovered for as long as possible. You may need a few hours to die. If the drugs you get are any good, it won't hurt.

Otherwise, suicide can be accomplished by drinking poison or slashing your wrists and neck. If you go the slashing route, make sure you really hack yourself to pieces. You'd be surprised how much blood you can lose and remain alive. On second thought, if you've gotten this far into the machine, you do know that.

Having a hypodermic needle can make so many things lethal. If something is thick (peanut butter?), you can inject it and cause a stroke or heart attack; otherwise, you might even resort to shooting up insecticide or gasoline. You might also ferment some of that nasty wine, then inject it all. Forget the air-injection method. To kill yourself that way, you have to inject way more than a few ccs of air bubbles.

In the holding cell, while on death watch, you may have one of the best opportunities of your life. If the doctor has decided to use Versed to calm you down you have access to a lethal drug right there.

He may have brought just enough for your 2.5-ml injection, but since you might get as many as three such shots before they kill you, he may have more of it on him. Five mls of Versed will anesthetize you, but one of the problems with the stuff is that it has to be calibrated very carefully since the difference between a therapeutic dose and a fatal dose is not that great. If you can lay your hands on 10 or 20 mls, you can shoot yourself up right there and die, or at least go into a coma, causing them the embarrassment and extra cost of keeping you alive or reviving you to kill you later.

"Cheating the hangman" is best done before the last minute. Unfortunately, most people are not willing to do themselves in until the last moment, when death is inevitable. Well, you know the statistics; after you've been on death row a few years you will have a pretty good idea of at least which six-month period will be your last.

Then again, suicide might have harsh consequences having nothing to do with the prison administration.

Taking Somebody With You

This may not be so smart. The other guys on death row don't need you to start letting the prison administrators set restrictions that make their lives even more miserable. On the other hand, if, on the way to the death chamber, you get a chance to kill a guard or even just hurt him bad — why not do it? Even if they beat the shit out of you in retaliation, it won't hurt for long.

If you manage to kill a pig on your way to the death chamber, you might even be able to win a *de facto* stay of execution so you can be tried for another capital crime and receive the death sentence again! Maybe you will be killed by the pigs while trying to save your ass — an interesting variation on cheating the hangman, as the state won't be able to kill you "cleanly" at all. It'll break down all the sterilization now in place to keep the procedure nice and cozy.

Once they've got you strapped to the chair, don't pay any attention to the audience, unless to say "'bye" to friends and loved ones. If you are a member of any political or religious group, then shout its slogan and say nothing more. This may inspire someone to do good one day.

And don't forget to pray!

6
An Afterword
On Forethought

In the end, no book can prepare you for the experiences that await you in the criminal justice machine. More importantly, no book can make that experience not hurt. A whole library of books cannot possibly be of help if you ever face a mean and vicious prosecutor/cop/judge or whomever. In the Appendix we provide a short list of recommended reading. Just remember the very first thing we discussed in this book: There Are No Loopholes.

There aren't even any built-in safeguards. There are no breaks at all.

In civil proceedings, you can find books about how to make your own will, write a contract, get a divorce or lots of other things. Some of them come with pre-printed tear-out sheets that save you from even doing the paperwork, not to mention the lawyer's fees.

Don't look for that here. You need an attorney.

One of the contributors to this effort you have here felt that some of the best advice about going to jail is to use your noodle a little bit so as to avoid going to jail in the first place.

Let's listen to him:

In the event you're engaged in activities that are "illegal," regardless of their nature, there are a few important things to bear in mind, which, if adhered to, will greatly reduce your chances of ever seeing the inside of a jail cell.

I speak of these "laws to live by" with all the authority of my own experience and the experience of over a decade of prison life — making careful study of the mistakes and slip-ups of literally hundreds of other prisoners during frank discussions on ways and means to avoid capture and our own inability to do so!

The rules of the game are simple and few:

1. Keep it to yourself! Approximately 90% of police work is based on gathering information — primarily from informers and programs such as "Crimestoppers" and the like. Why are the police so successful so often? The answer is quite simple — people like to talk, talk, talk! I'm not simply referring to confessions after arrest (dealt with elsewhere in the book), but instead I'm speaking about how many people cannot resist the temptation to tell the details of their illegal dealings and activities to others who are not involved; people who have no business whatsoever knowing the slightest thing about them.

The vast majority of people in prison today are there because they ran their mouths to friends, family, other prisoners and informers who, in turn, told someone else — most often the police!

The less said about a crime, the better. Best of all is to say nothing at all ever to anyone. Ever. If you've done something or are presently doing something illegal, no one besides those who are directly and necessarily involved should know about it. No one!

And those involved should know only as much as relates to the particular dealings you have with them. Remember the old "need to know" doctrine and follow it scrupulously. Just as you won't pry into their business, you will resist opening up to any sort of prying on their part.

If someone is not mature or reliable enough to understand being bluntly told, "That's none of your business," then you have picked a shaky crime associate. Dump him or her, as they are an extreme liability. Not only does losing that "partner" reduce your chances of being turned in to the police by some do-gooder or opportunist, it protects you from your old pal when he rats on you in a vain attempt to save himself.

As you have seen in this book, the suppression of evidence is essential. If a prosecutor can induce someone's associate to snitch against you, he has all he needs to destroy you. John Gotti, remember, was finally incarcerated because his associates turned on him.

Also realize that the information police rely on when investigating is not just limited to what you may say to others, but it includes your actions as well. And, as we all know, actions speak far louder than words.

For example, if you buy a new and expensive car with cash, it is a safe bet the dealer will immediately notify the authorities — and yes, they will investigate your sources of income for such a purchase. Even in the days before asset forfeiture, large amounts of cash were *de facto* evidence of wrong-doing. It's only worse today. Flashing around the fruits of your crime is particularly stupid. John Gotti, a supposed plumber, fucked up this way. So, if you're getting rich off crime, don't let your lifestyle betray you.

2.   Don't leave evidence laying around while committing a crime. This sounds so basic it's almost insulting, and yet, next to a confession, it's all the prosecutor really needs to nail you.

And it's hard not to leave evidence — there are so many types! There are fingerprints, bank money pouches, weapons, paperwork, audio and video tapes; the list can go on for pages. But whatever it is, it must be disposed of as quickly as possible after the fact and in such a way that its disposal attracts no attention. At a crime scene it pays to be thorough, because you probably won't get a chance to go back and do it a second time.

One prisoner I know used to do street robberies outside of prominent entertainment districts. When he was arrested the cops found his car contained hundreds of wallets, credit cards and the like, turning his bust for a single robbery into a bust for a slew of crimes — some of which were unknown to the cops! Simply stopping at a dumpster, wiping clean and pitching such evidence each night, would have saved this young man a lifetime of years behind bars.

When you break the law in such a way as robbing banks, murder, and the like, everything from bodies and weapons to clothing and bank paraphernalia should be immediately disposed of. If at all possible this should be done in such a way that none of the evidence can ever be discovered or recovered.

And, of course, tell no one the how and where!

An example of a fuck-up in this department was the father and son team that went across the midwest holding up banks using Reagan and Nixon masks. That made for nice headlines, but was rather stupid, since those same masks were used to tie them to each and every robbery. Had they only changed their M.O. a little bit each time (then destroyed the evidence and shut up), they would have only been directly linked with the robbery they were caught for.

It should be added that such a high-profile string of crimes mocks the police and they will spare no effort to find you.

The significance of this "golden rule" is that every bit of evidence laying around after the fact (or not properly disposed of) can and most likely will result in a bust, then a conviction, which probably means years of your life spent rotting in some cage.

Special attention should be paid to the realm of what is known as "white collar crimes," most of which involve a lot of paperwork that leads directly to you. In these cases you must guard against exposure even more carefully. If you are involved in an on-going scam such as embezzlement or constant theft, plan ahead. What happens if you get sick one day and can't show up to work on inventory day? Can your crime withstand a cursory examination? An extensive one? If not, then how will it look if you panic and drag yourself into work with a fever of 102?

Paperwork tends to linger. Photocopiers and carbonless copies have multiplied the amount of paperwork that then gets dispersed all around a business, or even to other cities. Its absence, too, may be just as conspicuous. Don't be so foolish as to leave evidence of your crime locked up in the boss's file cabinet.

And in these days of electronic data retrieval and other computer applications, your problems are even worse. If paper lingers, electrons are forever. On most computers simply "erasing" a file does nothing of the kind. Even programs that seem to obliterate all traces of a document or message are routinely defeated, and these days cops have learned something about computers. The FBI, especially, is quite adept at retrieving data that has been "destroyed" — this includes data from a hard drive dragged out of the remnants of a burned-out building!

And if paper multiplies fast, electronic information can and is duplicated hundreds of times over. Take a gander at spy and mental midget Oliver North. No matter how much he and his buddies "destroyed" electronic mail between themselves, even these "techno-spooks" couldn't get rid of it all.

There are precautions one can take to avoid all these problems, but they require forethought and diligence.

3. Get it right the first time. Whatever you do, realize that there's always time to plan and plot before the fact, and almost never time to correct mistakes once the deed is done. If you're planning to commit any crime, whether sticking up a store or growing some pot or anything else — don't just look at how easy it may seem, look at what could go wrong and how to prevent it.

Selling drugs out of your house? Don't be sneaky about it. Sell nightcrawlers. That way neighbors won't think twice about 5-minute visits at all hours of the day and night. And make sure you have nightcrawlers for sale, too!

The use of legitimate fronts and unwitting partners can keep you in business and out of jail. But you've got to use your brain! Envision the worst possible scenario, and then think how you might deal with it. Are you making a living shoplifting? Do you have a plausible story if you get caught walking out the door with something you didn't buy? Why don't you have a receipt? What if you only suspect you've been caught, and they're just waiting to nail you at the door? Can you dispose of the stolen item? Can you just brazenly walk up to the refund counter and try to "return" it?

Or are you going to stumble and fumble at your predicament? Have your spiel worked out so you won't contradict yourself or your crime partner's story. And if you conclude you must run for it, do you know where to run? What to do when you get there? Thinking ahead about all eventualities can save you from jail.

In summing up, it should be said that police are not superhuman, all-knowing crime-stoppers, nor do they have any crystal balls to look into while solving crimes. Instead, they do their work by careful use of investigative methods designed and proven to acquire and manipulate information.

By observing the above mentioned three "rules of the game" and otherwise keeping your wits about you, you can minimize the risk of arrest, substantially reduce the chance of conviction, and avoid going to jail. Just as no security system you encounter is foolproof (be it bank, computer, or even prison), the same applies to any system for avoiding the unfortunate eventuality of incarceration.

GET FREE! BE FREE! STAY FREE!

Appendix

A Few Recommended Books

Busted by the Feds (for defendants facing federal prosecution, with specific guideline information for all drug cases), by Larry Fassler, Southwest Legal Services, Tucson, AZ 1992, 1993 (revised).

Available also in Spanish, this book deals with the complicated but all-important issues surrounding the infamous federal sentencing guidelines. In addition to some plea-bargaining strategies and explanations of mitigating and aggravating circumstances, this book can also serve as a guide to predict what your sentence will be, according to your crime.

The strict categories outlined by the federal government are a double-edged sword, so this book gives insight into certain "thresholds" that may shift your classification enough to make many many years of difference.

It also gives information on which prison you're likely to go to and even has a map of every federal facility along with information about its capacity, overcrowding, etc.

Spectre of Forfeiture, by Judy Osborne, Access Unlimited, Frazier Park, CA, 1991. An indispensable book for anyone facing the confiscation of everything they own through asset forfeiture as sanctified at both state and federal levels. Judy's story is complete, and reading it can give you a fighting chance to evade having your life torn apart by being fined essentially "everything you got now and for the rest of your life" — a form of punishment that's become popular over the years.

Remember, the state can do this without convicting you. They can do it even without arresting you. Anyone can be attacked by this. Don't be ambushed.

Green Panthers Action Manual, 1991. This book assumes the reader is already under attack by the government. This manual details ways to organize and effectively resist an occupational government. Police surveillance, search methods and other tactics are described from cop sources.

Voices Behind the Wall, by John P. Farrell, Henry Holt & Co., NY, 1986. This book is a collection of stories, anecdotes, quotes and other verbalized thoughts of prisoners in maximum-security prisons. The author, who heard them in his capacity as prison psychologist, has rendered them just as he heard them without editorial comment. The result is a book that will terrorize your soul and give you a glimpse of life in prison.

Of course, there are a lot of books describing the horrors of prison life, and almost all of them have something to offer. Jessica Mitford's *Cruel and Usual Punishment* comes to mind. Read anything you can on prison. I only cite the above book because it is the most succinct in describing the atmosphere of prison.

Post-Release Assistance Programs for Prisoners: A National Directory, by Anthony J. Bosoni, McFarland & Company, Jefferson, North Carolina, 1992.

Rape Materials

Practical information on audio tapes made by ex-prisoners specifically for men confined in jail are available from The Prisoners Rape Education Project. On a 27-minute audio tape called *An Ounce of Prevention*, the men use common slang and feature speakers from a variety of ethnic and racial backgrounds. On the tape, they try to outline the range of situations confronting prisoners. Emphasizing the problem of sexual assault, they suggest assault-avoidance tactics. The tape is intended for use in prisoner-orientation programs.

There is another tape, this one 90 minutes, called *Becoming a Survivor,* emphasizing survival issues for victims of sexual assault in confinement, along with a 46-page manual for staff *(Overview for Jail/Prisoner Administrators and Staff).* Although it is written for prison staff, it is useful for anyone interested in the problem of prison rape. It has up-to-date information on institutional legal responsibilities, the complications posed by AIDS, the first published description of Male Rape Trauma Syndrome among prisoners, a full description of "protective pairing" (hooking up), a bibliography, a list of available resources and excerpts from a key court decision.

Please pre-pay all orders. The first tape, *An Ounce of Prevention,* is $5 plus $3 for shipping. The second tape, *Becoming a Survivor,* offers comfort and encouragement to a prisoner who has been raped so that "he can become a survivor (and learn) that common myths about rape and manhood or sexuality have no actual basis in fact." This tape costs $8 plus $3 shipping, but is available for free to any prisoner who has already suffered from sexual assault.

Order from:

The Safer Society of Program and Press
PO Box 340
Brandon, VT 05733-0340

You may also write:

SPR
PO Box 2713
Manhattenville Station
New York, NY 10027

More information on Stop Prisoner Rape can be obtained from a small organization dealing with the issue by writing:
SPR (address listed above).

Criminal Justice Publications

Bulldozer
PO Box 5052, Station A
Toronto, Ontario M5W 1W4
CANADA

Bi-monthly tabloid paper on prison conditions in the U.S. and elsewhere. Free to prisoners. Postage to Canada is 40 cents.

Coalition For Prisoners Rights Newsletter
Box 1911
Santa Fe, NM 87504
Newsletter on politics and prison conditions free to prisoners. Volunteer staff, no pen pals. Will try to publish short statements about conditions where you are.

Convictions
PO Box 1749
Corvallis, OR 97339-1749

Criminal Procedure Project
Georgetown Law Journal
600 New Jersey Ave NW
Washington, DC 20001
Information on criminal procedure, *habeus corpus* relief and prisoners' rights. $5. Ask about free copies of their special issue of the *Georgetown Law Journal.*

Fortress Economy
AFSC
1501 Cherry St.
Philadelphia, PA 19102
New booklet on U.S. prison system as source of cheap labor. Free to prisoners.

Fortune News
Inmate Subscriptions
39 West 19th St.
New York, NY 10011
Quarterly magazine for prisoners. Free to prisoners.

Kick It Over
Box 5811, Station A
Toronto, Ontario M5W 1P2
CANADA
An anti-authoritarian magazine with a feminist/ecological perspective. Free to prisoners. Postage to Canada is 40 cents.

National Prison Project Journal
ACLU
1875 Connecticut Ave. NW
Washington, DC 20009
Prisoner rights news and case law. Reduced cost to prisoners: $2 per year.

Odyssey
PO Box 14
Dedham, MA 02026
Creative alternatives in criminal justice. $3 per issue for prisoners, or $10 for a four-issue subscription.

Outlook On Justice
AFSC, Outlook On Justice
2161 Mass. Ave.
Cambridge, MA 02140
A prisoner support newsletter produced by the American Friends Service Committee. $2 to prisoners. Pen pal space.

Prison Journal
Institute of the Humanities
Simon Fraser University
Burnaby, BC V5A 1S6
CANADA
Prison literature, printed once a year, free to prisoners. Postage to Canada is 40 cents.

Prison News Service
PO Box 5052, Station A
Toronto, Ontario M5W 1W4
CANADA
News and letters from prisoners — free! 40 cents postage to Canada.

Prisoner Legal News
PO Box 1684
Lake Worth, FL 33460
Excellent prisoner newsletter. Send donation of stamps or money for subscription.

Reality Now
Box 6326, Station A
Toronto, Ontario M5W 1P7
CANADA
Anarchist news journal covering prison, Native American, and other issues. Free to prisoners. Postage to Canada is 40 cents.

Resistance
PO Box 790, Station A
Vancouver, BC V6C 2N6
CANADA
Postage to Canada is 40 cents.

Pen Pals

The Enchanted Mailbox
International Pen Pals
136 Newberry Rd.
Nowell, NJ 07731

Friendship Bulletin
PO Box 1716
Chula Vista, CA 92021

The Other Side
300 West Aspley St.
Philadelphia, PA 19144

Prison Fellowship
Inmate Request Form
PO Box 17500 (PS/G)
Washington, DC 20041

Prison Outreach
495 Albion Ave.
Cincinnati, OH 45246
A quarterly newsletter for any prisoner — funded by a Catholic organization.

Prison Penpals
Box 1217
Cincinnati, OH 45201

Sarakinos Help By Correspondence Foundation
61 Antistaseos St.
PO Box 152
31 Athens
GREECE
Retired individuals who would like to write to prisoners. Postage to Greece is 58 cents.

Notes about placing ads (Prisoners Writing Prisoners): When you place a pen pal ad, it is a good idea to say whether or not you can write to other prisoners. Just because your joint lets you write to other prisoners doesn't mean other joints do, so don't assume that another prisoner isn't interested in writing just because you don't get an answer. He or she may not have even seen the letter. As you know, they change the "rules" all the time, and break them when they feel like it (when they are worried about how much you are enjoying writing each other) (smile).

Books, Etc.

African-American Images
9204 Commercial, Suite 308
Chicago, IL 60617

Books Not Bars
New Society Publishers
4527 Springfield Ave
Philadelphia, PA 19143

Books for Prisoners
c/o Left Bank Books
92 Pike St.
Seattle, WA 98101

Prisoner Literature Project
Bound Together Books
1369 Haight St.
San Francisco, CA 94117

Prison Library Project
976 Foothill Blvd. #128
Claremont, CA 91711

Prison Book Program
92 Green St.
Jamaica Plain, MA 02130
(Used (donated) books only. Volunteers are 4-6 months behind. No
books to these states: KS, NE, IA, MI, OR, CA.)

The above programs send books to state and federal prisoners
throughout the country at no charge. You may request reading material
on a particular subject. Sometimes they are 4-6 months behind in filling
requests, so please be patient. Not a source for pen pals.

Association for Research and Enlightenment
PO Box 595
Virginia Beach, VA 23451

Aurora Press
PO Box 573
Santa Fe, NM 87504
Books on health, spiritual growth, psychological growth.

Center for Spiritual Awareness
PO Box 7
Lakemont, GA 30552
Books sent free to prisoners on metaphysics and Kriyer Yoga. Monthly
publication *Truth Journals*.

Healing Tao Center
PO Box 1194
Huntington, NY 11743
Books on Taoist Yoga methods.

Mostazafan Foundation of NY
c/o Book Distribution Program
500 Fifth Ave., 34th Floor
New York, NY 10110
Free Korans and other Islamic materials to Muslims.

Prison Ashram Project
Rte 1 Box 201-N
Durham, NC 27705
Free newsletter.

Whole Gay Catalog
Lambda Rising
Dept. 157
1625 Conn. Ave. NW
Washington, DC 20009
$2.00

Legal Information/Self Help Resources

ACLU Handbook: The Rights of Prisoners
ACLU
132 West 43rd St.
New York, NY 10036
A guide to the legal rights of prisoners, parolees, and pre-trial detainees.
Contains citations. $5 to prisoners.

Blackstone School of Law
PO Box 790906
Dallas, TX 75379-0906
Lost cost paralegal course by mail. Covers principles of civil and criminal law.

Freedom
3521 Mountain Rd
Haymarket, VA 22069
Low cost paralegal services.

Henry George Institute
121 East 30th St.
New York, NY 10016
Home study course in economics. Small charge for materials, no tuition cost.

Jailhouse Lawyer's Manual
Columbia Human Rights Law Review
West 116th St., Box 25
New York, NY 10027
A new (3rd) edition is now available; $13 for prisoners.

Legal Bulletins
Lewisburg Prison Project
Box 128
Lewisburg, PA 17837
Write for FREE catalog of federal prisoners rights.

Native American Rights Fund
Legal Review
1506 Broadway
Boulder, CO 80302

NLADA Directory
1625 K St. NW, 8th Floor
Washington, DC 20006
National listing of free legal aid services.

Photoduplication Service
Library of Congress
Washington, DC 20540
Copies of manuscripts, prints, photographs, maps, etc. are available on request from the Photoduplication Service. (Copyrighted materials cannot be copied without special permission.) Fees vary according to the request. Write to the above address for order forms and price lists.

Photograph Reproduction
Color Lab
8 Burnett Ave.
Maplewood, NJ 07040
Send for price list — cheap reproduction of photos.

Post-conviction Remedies: A Self-Help Manual
Oceana Press
75 Main St.
Dobbs Ferry, NY 10522
Outlines the procedures for challenging convictions. $16.50.

Rules of Criminal Procedure/Federal Rules of Evidence
Judiciary Committee
House of Representatives
Washington, DC 20515
Limited number of free copies of U.S. Constitution, *How Laws are Made,* Federal Rules of Evidence, Civil Procedure, Criminal Procedure, and Appellate Procedure. Also available for a fee from:
Superintendent of Documents
Government Printing Office
Congressional Sales Office
Washington, DC 20402, write for information.

Self-Help Litigation Manual
Oceana Press
75 Main St.
Dobbs Ferry, NY 10522
This excellent book includes chapters on legal research, how the legal system works, an overview of prisoners rights, how to litigate in federal courts, parole, federal post-conviction remedies, law-library requirements, civil-rights forms and MORE! Available to prisoners for $20.

West Publishing Company
PO Box 64526
St. Paul, MN 55164-0526
1-800-328-9352
Publishes many different law books, most of them expensive. Call or write for information and a free copy of *West's Law Finder: A Legal Research Manual.* They also publish *Corrections and Prisoners Rights In A Nutshell* ($16.95), which provides an overview of the sentencing process, the status of pre-trial detainees and convicted offenders, prisoners rights and responsibilities, and restoration of rights for released offenders; and *Criminal Procedure In A Nutshell* ($16.95), which concentrates on constitutional criminal procedures and their limitations. The 4th, 6th and 14th Amendments are heavily covered. Includes a table of cases.

Prisoner Support

American Friends Service Committee
AFSC has 6 regional criminal justice offices. Each is a good resource
for information pertaining to the community, state and region in which
that office is located. AFSC regional offices are:

AFSC Criminal Justice Program
405 14th St. #813
Oakland, CA 94612
(415) 836-2144

AFSC Criminal Justice Program
1414 Hill St.
Ann Arbor, MI 48104
(313) 761-8283

AFSC Criminal Justice Program
972 Walnut St., 6th Floor
Newark, NJ 07102
(201) 643-3079

AFSC Justice Program
2161 Mass Ave
Cambridge, MA 02140
(617) 442-9563

AFSC Community Relations
915 Salem Ave
Dayton, OH 45406
(513) 278-4225

AFSC Mediation Center
Meeting House, 137-16 Northern Blvd.
Flushing, NY 11354
(718) 939-1300

AFSC Undocumented Refugee Project
1205 Sunset Dr.
South Miami, FL 33143
Information for immigration detainees.

American Indian Gays and Lesbians
Box 10229
Minneapolis, MN 55458

Bayou La Rose
302 N. J St. #3
Tacoma, WA 98403
Native American prisoner support.

Behind The Walls
5 Star Press
PO Box 4167
Halfmoon, NY 12065
Prisoner support publication formed to assist prisoners in the United States and abroad. Pen pals, legal news reporting, library services, counseling, exposing abuse, outside contacts, writing projects. $5 to prisoners (stamps ok).

CLEP (College Level Examination Program)
CN 6600
Princeton, NJ 08541-6600
If you feel you have acquired knowledge of a subject without the usual formal education, you may take the college level examination, and, with satisfactory test results, can obtain college credit. CLEP makes these examinations available to prisoners. Write to the above address for a catalogue of test subjects offered and for information about making the necessary arrangements.

Coalition For Jewish Prisoners Service
c/o Martin Hockberg
1640 Rhode Island Ave NW
Washington, DC 20036

Contact Referral Center, Inc.
PO Box 81826
Lincoln, NE 68501
This national information and referral service for prisoners attempts to link people with resources in the community that can be of help upon release, such as drug and alcohol programs, employment, housing, counseling and other services. Three to four months before your parole hearing or expected release date, write to the above address for a request form. On this form you will identify the state you will be paroled to and the referrals you require. You will be required to pay $10 when you send back your form. Ask them for a copy of their booklet *Survival Sourcebook* about finding a place to live and job hunting.

CURE (Citizens United for the Rehabilitation of Errants)
CURE's work focuses on analysis of prison issues and on working with the friends and families of prisoners. All letters answered with short responses. No collect calls.
National office:
CURE
11 15th St. NE #6
Washington, DC 20002
(202) 543-8399

Florida:
CURE
c/o Linda McCray
4000 SW 47th St. F8
Gainesville, FL 32608

Indiana:
CURE
Federal Prison Chapter
PO Box 6176
Terre Haute, IN 47802

Louisiana:
CURE
PO Box 181
Baton Rouge, LA 70821

Massachusetts:
CURE
24 Laurel St.
Somerville, MA 02143

Michigan:
CURE
309 Seymour
Lansing, MI 48933

Missouri:
CURE
PO Box 29041
St. Louis, MO 63112

New York:
CURE
PO Box 893
Highland, NY 12528

Ohio:
CURE
PO Box 5022
Cleveland, OH 44101-0022

Pennsylvania:
CURE
1034 E. Sedgwick
Philadelphia, PA 19150-2227

Texas:
CURE
PO Box 12623
Austin, TX

Virginia:
CURE
PO Box 19453
Alexandria, VA 22320

Wisconsin:
CURE
PO Box 9452
Madison, WI 53715-0452

Double Image
c/o F. Rivera
127 Irving Ave
Brooklyn, NY 11237
TV/TS information.

Families Against Mandatory Minimums (FAMM)
2000 L Street NW
Washington, DC 20036

Freedom Now
59 East Van Buren #1400
Chicago, IL 60605
Support for political prisoners.

Friends Outside
116 East San Luis St.
Salinas, CA 93901
(408) 758-2733
Support for prisoners and families of prisoners. Write and ask if there's a group in your area.

Inside Journal
Prison Fellowship
PO Box 16429
Washington, DC 20041-6429

Institute of Islamic Information and Education
PO Box 41129
Chicago, IL 60641-0129
Distributes information about the Nation of Islam.

Justice Watch
932 Dayton St.
Cincinnati, OH 45214
Grassroots prisoners' rights group. Newsletter available to prisoners.

League for Lesbian & Gay Prisoners (LLGP)
1202 E Pike St., Suite 1044
Seattle, WA 98122-3934
A new network for lesbians and gay men in and out of prison. Write for information.

Minority Prison Project
c/o Rev. John Prowett
1308 Jefferson Ave
Memphis, TN 38104-2012
Information and support for lesbians, gay men, and bisexuals in prison; referrals and penpals.

MOMS (Mothers Opposed to Maltreatment of Service Members)
8525 Black Haw Court
Frederick, MD 21701
(301) 662-7643
Legal services, newsletter, support for military prisoners, veteran benefits.

NAACP Prison Program
4805 Mt. Hope Dr.
Baltimore, MD 21215
Education, health care, ex-offender rights, job placement & counseling.

National Coalition Against The Death Penalty
1325 G St. NW, Lower Level B
Washington, DC 20005
(202) 797-7090

National Home Study Council
1601 18th St. NW
Washington, DC 20009
Information about academic and job training schools that offer home/prison courses by mail. Write for a directory of schools and courses.

National Lawyers Guild
55 Avenue of the Americas
New York, NY 10013

This organization does not take on prisoners' legal cases, but they need to be reminded that the criminal justice system has serious problems. If you have an extra stamp, drop them a line. Don't expect a reply.

National Legal Aid And Defender Association
1625 K St., 8th Floor
Washington, DC 20006
Referrals to legal programs and services in your area. No direct services.

The National Prison Project of the ACLU
1875 Connecticut Ave NW
Washington, DC 20009
(202) 234-4830
The National Prison Project of the American Civil Liberties Union handles litigation on prison and jail conditions. They are NOT a resource for handling individual convictions or problems unless related to conditions of confinement. Your local ACLU affiliate is a good place to begin regarding individual problems. Write for the address of your local chapter.

National Task Force On Prostitution
Box 26354
San Francisco, CA 94126
Works to discriminalize prostitution.

NGLTF Anti-Violence Project
1517 U St. NW
Washington, DC 20009
The National Gay And Lesbian Task Force is keeping a file of incidents of violence against lesbians and gay men. NGLTF needs to know details about: verbal harassment or physical assault. NGLTF does not provide any legal services.

Office of Correctional Education
U.S. Dept. of Education
400 Maryland Ave SW
Washington, DC 20202

Write for information about educational grants to federal and state prisoners.

Offender Aid and Restoration
301 Park Drive
Severna Park, MD 21146
Services for offenders, ex-offenders and their families.

PEN American Center
568 Broadway
New York, NY 10012
Prison writers may send for a free bulletin to find out about publications that want to receive writings from prisoners (poetry, fiction, non-fiction or drama), writing contests for prisoners, and tips on how to get your writing into print.

Pennsylvania Prison Society
3 North 2nd St.
Philadelphia, PA 19106
Advocacy and support for prisoners and families in Pennsylvania.

People Organized To Stop Rape of Prisoners
Box 632
Ft. Bragg, CA 95437
Newsletter, support for rape survivors.

The Poetry Wall
Cathedral of St. John the Divine
1047 Amsterdam Ave
New York, NY 10025
Accepts poetry of all kinds to display to the public in the cathedral and invites anyone to correspond with inmates whose poetry is displayed.

Prisoners' Rights Advocacy Centers Of America
204 Elmo Ave
San Antonio, TX 78225
Offers assistance with legal work.

The Fortune Society
39 West 19th St.
New York, NY 10011

Prison Dharma Network
PO Box 912
Astor Station
Boston, MA 02123-0912
Non-sectarian Buddhist support network for prisoners. Provides correspondent meditation instructors, free Buddhist meditation books, and Dharma center contacts.

MGNA
PO Box 566
Ojai, CA 93024-0566
Write for information about meditation course.

Prisoners Union
PO Box 1019
Sacramento, CA 95812-1019
California prisoner support newsletter and referral service. They also distribute "Inside/Out Press Manuals" which are legal self-help manuals. Write for free catalog.

Prisoner Visitation and Support
1501 Cherry St.
Philadelphia, PA 19102
(215) 241-7117
PVS visits only federal and military prisoners wanting visits. PVS offers friendship, regular visits, study materials, helps with family communications and legal referrals, and writes letters of recommendation to parole boards.

Renaissance Education Association, Inc.
PO Box 552
King of Prussia, PA 19406
TV/TS support.

Southern Prisoners Defense Committee
185 Walton St. NW
Atlanta, GA 30303
Death penalty work.

Tower Press
410 Penn St.
Holidaysburg, PA 16648
Publishes writing by prisoners.

Transsexuals In Prison (TIP)
c/o Rev. John Prowett
1308 Jefferson Ave
Memphis, TN 38104-2012
TV/TS information and support; newsletter and penpals.

Universal Suffrage
Box 35
Alto, GA 30510

Safer Sex And Drug Use Guidelines

We offer these guidelines for all of us who are making decisions about sex and drug use in the midst of the AIDS epidemic. This information is available in Spanish. For a copy, write to: Prison Book Program, 92 Green St., Jamaica Plain, MA 02130.

HIV is a virus widely thought to be a cause of AIDS. The highest concentrations of HIV are found in blood and sperm/cum. So it's important to avoid any way HIV-infected blood or sperm/cum can get from one person's body into another person's bloodstream.

Fucking (up the ass or cunt) without a condom (rubber, safe) and sharing needles account for almost all the documented cases of HIV passing from one person's body into another's. Oral sex (licking/sucking your partner's cunt/cock) without a condom or plastic/rubber protection accounts for a very few documented cases of HIV transmission. Other ways of transmitting HIV that have not been documented but which could be risky include: fisting or finger-fucking (putting fingers or hands into a cunt or asshole), rimming (licking/sucking assholes), deep kissing, sharing unclean dildos.

The idea here is that any way HIV-infected blood or sperm/cum gets from one person into another involves risk. For example, HIV could be transmitted if a person with a cut on their hand fistfucked his or her partner and caused bleeding in their partner's ass or cunt.

How to Play Safer

Only you can decide what risks you are willing to take. Some people use safe-sex practices with all their partners. Other people make decisions about the risks they are willing to take based on their own and their partner's sexual and drug use history and/or HIV status (whether or not either of you has tested positive for HIV). People also make decisions based on how comfortable they feel talking about safe sex in a particular situation. If you and your partner have not talked about past practices and/or HIV status, don't make assumptions.

Use a condom (rubber, safe) when fucking. On the condoms, use water-based lubricants like KY. Oil-based lubricants like Crisco, Vaseline, and bay oil may make the condom break. Use a condom (rubber, safe) when sucking dick. If you don't use a condom, don't let your partner cum in your mouth and don't cum in your partner's mouth. If HIV-infected cum or pre-cum gets in your mouth, it may get in your bloodstream through cuts in your gums or sores in your mouth. Use plastic/rubber protection (like Saran Wrap or dental dams) when licking/sucking a woman's cunt, especially if she is having her period. Menstrual blood and secretions from vaginal infections have more HIV than healthy vaginal secretions and piss. Plastic/rubber protection may also be used for rimming (licking/sucking assholes). Use plastic/rubber gloves for fisting or finger-fucking, especially if you have any sores or cuts on your hands. Keep sperm/cum and blood (including menstrual blood and blood drawn from tattooing, piercing, cutting or shaving) out of your cunt, asshole, mouth, or breaks in your skin. If you share dildos, vibrators or other sex toys, use a new condom each time or clean the toys with hydrogen peroxide or, if you don't have any, soap and water.

Massage, hugging, dirty talk, butch/femme role-playing, masturbation (by yourself, with a partner, or a group) and other activities that don't let blood or sperm/cum into your bloodstream are safe. Alcohol, poppers or other drugs may lower your ability to think clearly. Many people have reported that they have been unable to have safe sex after getting high. Good nutrition, lots of rest, exercise and not abusing alcohol and other drugs may help you fight all illness, including AIDS.

IV Drug Use

Don't share works (needles, syringes, droppers, spoons, cottons or cookers)!

If you must share or re-use works, clean them before and after each injection as follows: dip needle and works into bleach, draw up and release three times. In an emergency, rubbing alcohol or vodka can be used instead of bleach. Or you can boil works (that aren't plastic) in water for at least 15 minutes. (Use a fresh solution each time you clean your works.)

For more information about AIDS:

Aids And Drug Use Information
Fortune Society
D. Dawood
39 West 19th St.
New York, NY 10011

Aids And Prisons Pamphlet
ACLU National Prison Project
1616 P St. NW
Washington, DC 20036
Free!

AIDS In Prison Project
Correctional Association of NY
135 E 15th St.
New York, NY 10003
For prisoners in New York State. Write for information.

AIDS Information Line
Call 1-800-342-7514 for talk and facts.
Call 1-800-221-7044 for info pamphlets. These calls are free! Spread these numbers around.

AIDS Legal Referral Panel
Box 1983
San Francisco, CA 94101
(415) 864-8186

If you are a person with AIDS or ARC, this organization can provide you with legal help — either at a reduced cost or for free.

Alianza
PO Box 53396
Washington, DC 20009
Informacion sobre SIDA. Un proyecto del communidad latino-americano.

AIDS/HIV in Correctional Settings
U.S. Conference of Mayors
1620 I St. NW
Washington, DC 20006
AIDS information exchange is a very useful account of the ground-breaking policies in the Philadelphia jail system. Free to prisoners.

The Body Positive
208 West 13th St.
New York, NY 10011
Information for HIV-positive people.

Criminalization Of The AIDS Epidemic
National Lawyers Guild AIDS Network
558 Capp St.
San Francisco, CA 94110
Article that talks about mandatory testing and AIDS. $2.25

Gay American Indians Aids Project
333 Valencia St. #207
San Francisco, CA 94103
AIDS awareness and prevention program. Provides services for Native Americans with AIDS/ARC/HIV+.

Inmate To Inmate
Gilbert Serrano
c/o PWA C
31 W. 26th St.
New York, NY 10010

A brochure developed by a prisoner in the NYS prison system addresses AIDS and HIV issues such as "How Long Do I Got (To Live)?" He hopes to distribute them nationally.

National Commission On AIDS
1730 K St. NW, Suite 815
Washington, DC 20006
Write for a copy of report on AIDS in U.S. prisons.

National Institute of Justice
1600 Research Blvd.
Rockville, MD 20850
NIJ publishes several free pamphlets: *AIDS in Correctional Facilities*, and *AIDS in Probation and Parole Services*.

HIV Prison Project
New York City Commission on Human Rights
40 Rector St.
New York, NY 10006
Information and assistance with discrimination and treatment issues. Telephone hotline: (212) 233-5560 (Collect ok, se habla espanol).

Nutrition Information for People With AIDS and ARC
Dept. of Public Health
101 Grove St., Rm. 118
San Francisco, CA 94102

People With AIDS Coalition Newsline
31 West 26th St.
New York, NY 10011
A monthly newsletter free to people with AIDS who can't afford it, including prisoners. Free pen pal listing.

Prison AIDS Resource Center
PO Box 2155
Vacaville, CA 95696-8155
Information, support.

Prisoners With AIDS — Rights Advocacy Group (PWA — RAG)
PO Box 2161
Jonesboro, GA 30237
Information and support. Write for free newsletter.

National Prison Hospice Association
PO Box 58
Boulder, CO 80306-0058
Assists in the development of hospice/palliative care programs for dying prisoners and their families.

News/News Analysis

Breakthrough
PO Box 14422
San Francisco, CA 94114
Journal of the Prairie Fire Organizing Committee. Info on political prisoners and prisoners of war. Free to prisoners.

Burning Spear Newspaper
794 McArthur St.
Oakland, CA 94605

Gay Community News
GCN Lesbian and Gay Prisoner Project
25 West St.
Boston, MA 02111
Please note: Due to financial problems, GCN has suspended publication, and the prisoner project has suspended operation. Subscription and pen pal ads are not available at this time. Restructuring and fundraising are under way, and the paper hopes to return soon.

Industrial Worker
3435 North Sheffield Ave #202
Chicago, IL 60657

Love and Rage
Box 3, Prince St. Station
New York, NY 10012

Anarchist monthly free to prisoners. Prisoner letters and news.

MIM Notes
4521 Campus Dr. #535
Irvine, CA 92715
The official newsletter of the Maoist International Movement, with a section on prison news. Free to prisoners. They also provide free Maoist and general political books for prisoners.

The Militant
14 Charles Lane
New York, NY 10014
Socialist Newspaper $12/year.

NAMBLA Bulletin
c/o Rock Thatcher
4730 E Indian School Rd #120-263
Phoenix, AZ 85018
Bulletin of the North American Man/Boy Love Association. Free to persons imprisoned for sex with minors.

The People's Daily World
235 West 23rd St.
New York, NY 10011
Published by the U.S. Communist Party. $10/year.

Project 1313
PO Box 1313
Lawrence, KS 66044
Information on anarchist political prisoners. Free to prisoners.

The Shadow
c/o The Shadow Press
PO Box 20298
New York, NY 10009

Theosophical Society In America
1926 Main St.
PO Box 270
Wheaton, IL 60189-0270
The Light Within (quarterly newsletter). $5 to prisoners.

Torch/La Torcha
PO Box 3
New York, NY 10012-0001

Unity
PO Box 29293
Oakland, CA 94604
Half in English, half in Spanish, good photography, addresses, anti-racism in an "upbeat" way. Free to prisoners.

Worker's World
Prisoner Subscriptions
46 West 21st St.
New York, NY 10010

Notes About News Publications:
   Letters to The Editor: Prisoners have just as much right as anyone to write letters to the editors of their local newspapers. Take advantage of this right regularly (if you have any postage), even though they may not always publish your letters; sometimes they will, and this may help readers understand more about what prison is about.

Journals of Stories, Poems, Essays

Factsheet Five
c/o R. Seth Friedman
PO Box 170099
San Francisco, CA 94117-0099
Review of alternative press publications. Write for info about prisoners' subscriptions.

Primary Concern
Marc Fisher, Editor
234 Lloyd Lane
Philadelphia, PA 19151
A magazine of music, photos, fun and social conscience, free to prisoners.

SIDDHA Meditation Prison Project
SYDA Foundation
Box 600
South Fallsburg, NY 12779
A correspondence course free to prisoners. No penpals.

SIPAPU
c/o Noel Peattie
Rt. 1, Box 216
Winters, CA 95694
Biannual alternative political publication. Free to prisoners.

Index

YOU WILL ALSO WANT TO READ:

☐ **76041 The Outlaw's Bible,** *by E.X. Boozhle.* The best "jailhouse" law book ever published — for people on the outside who want to stay there. This is a real life civics lesson for citizen lawbreakers: how to dance on the fine line between freedom and incarceration, how to tiptoe the tightrope of due process. Covers detention, interrogation, searches and seizures. The only non-violent weapon available for those on the wrong side of the law. *1985, 5½ x 8½, 336 pp, Index, soft cover.* **$16.95.**

☐ **40070 Surviving In Prison,** *by Harold S. Long.* A disturbing account of life behind bars. The author has spent the last ten years in prison. He describes how prisons are run: the penal code and the cellblock code. He takes you out in the yard and into the hole. He explains why rehabilitation programs fail. And he reveals what is required to survive the personal degradation, brutality and humiliation found in contemporary American prisons. *1990, 8½ x 11, 122 pp, soft cover.* **$14.95.**

☐ **40066 Escape From Controlled Custody,** *by Tony Lesce.* Right now, there are people held captive all over the world. Some of them will try to escape. A few will succeed. This book takes you captive to show you what it's like. You'll learn to make knives from toothbrushes and printing presses from shoes. You'll follow prisoners through tunnels and over walls. Along the way, you'll hear about some of the great escapes: acts of bravery and cunning that stir the human spirit. *1990, 5½ x 8½, 144 pp, Illustrated, Index, soft cover.* **$12.95.**

☐ **40071 The Big House, How American Prisons Work,** *by Tony Lesce.* This book is a *thorough examination* of how prisons work: how you house, feed, and control thousands of violent, angry people. It examines the prison system from all sides: the inmates, the guards, the politicians, the taxpayers. And it takes a gritty look at issues like capital punishment, psychosurgery, riot control and dealing with the sexual needs of prisoners. *1991, 8½ x 11, 184 pp, Illustrated, Index, soft cover.* **$19.95.**

GTP98

Loompanics Unlimited
PO Box 1197
Port Townsend, WA 98368

Please send me the books I have checked above. I have enclosed $_____ which includes $4.95 for shipping and handling of books totaling $20. (Include $1 for each additional $20 in books ordered.) Washington residents include 7.9% sales tax.

Name _____

Address _____

City/State/Zip _____

We accept Visa and MasterCard. To place a credit card order *only*, call 1-800-380-2230, Monday through Friday, 8am to 4pm, PST.

YOU WILL ALSO WANT TO READ:

☐ **58100 How To Survive Federal Prison Camp, A Guidebook For Those Caught Up In The System,** *by Clive Sharp, with an Introduction by Claire Wolfe.* Author Clive Sharp, a recent graduate of the American federal prison camp system has compiled an essential guidebook that is designed to make a prison camp resident's life bearable. Sharp provides tips that range from pre-sentencing considerations and making prior arrangements, medical and dental advice, realities from day-to-day existence, various camp regulations, and how to choose preferable camps and work assignments, on through how to deal with halfway houses, supervised release, and getting a post-camp job and restoring your civil rights. Absolutely essential reading for anyone who is going to do time in a federal prison camp. *1997, 5½ x 8½, 170 pp, illustrated, soft cover.* $16.95.

☐ **76059 How To Clear Your Adult And Juvenile Criminal Records,** *by William Rinehart.* Author William Rinehart is well-qualified to dispense advice on how to clear one's criminal records. He had two felony convictions and over 30 misdemeanors to his credit, before he took the necessary steps to cleanse his adult and juvenile records. Now Rinehart's criminal records are purged of serious offenses, he has all the rights and privileges that American citizens are meant to enjoy under the Constitution, and he shares his hard-earned secrets in this unique sourcebook, which contains never-before revealed step-by-step instructions, along with example forms and comprehensive state-by-state lists of the statutes and laws which must be cited. If a nagging criminal record is holding your back, this book can change your life! *1997, 5½ x 8½, 112 pp, illustrated, soft cover.* $12.95.

☐ **85158 How To Avoid A Drunk Driving Conviction,** *by Judge X.* A 20-year veteran of the bench, Judge X reveals everything drinkers must know about drunk driving and the law: What to do at a traffic stop; How to beat a DUI; How to hand judges, lawyers, cops and the MADD crusaders; 100 rules for the road; And much more, including a pocket kit for the drinking driver. Lawyers charge thousands of dollars for the information presented in this book. Don't leave home without it. *1993, 5½ x 8½, 168 pp, soft cover.* $14.95.

_____ GTP98

Loompanics Unlimited
PO Box 1197
Port Townsend, WA 98368

Please send me the books I have checked above. I have enclosed $_____ which includes $4.95 for shipping and handling of books totaling $20. (Include $1 for each additional $20 in books ordered.) Washington residents include 7.9% sales tax.

Name _____

Address _____

City/State/Zip_____

We accept Visa and MasterCard. To place a credit card order *only*, call 1-800-380-2230, Monday through Friday, 8am to 4pm, PST.

YOU WILL ALSO WANT TO READ: